*Sanity for All
in the
21st Century...*

Sanity for All in the 21st Century...

REFLECTIONS OF A FIN DE SIÈCLE FEMINIST

Elayne Clift

To order additional copies of this book, contact:
Xlibris Corporation
1-888-795-4274
www.Xlibris.com
Orders@Xlibris.com
16290

Contents

ACKNOWLEDGMENTS 17

I

BEATING THE BUSHES AND OTHER POLITICAL ACTS

SEX, LIES, AND SANDBOX POLITICS 21

BEGGING YOUR PARDON 25

SAY WHAT? 29

UP IN ARMS 31

CONSERVATIVE OR MEAN-SPIRITED?
THE FIRST 100+ DAYS 33

POLITICAL PERSUASION OR
PERSONALITY DISORDER? 37

YOU CAN SAY THAT AGAIN! 41

WHERE IS HEALTH CARE ON
THE RADAR SCREEN? 45

THE POLITICAL MESSIAH 49

IS THERE AN ARTIST IN
THE HOUSE . . . OR SENATE? 51

RECALLING OUR FLAWS ON
    THE FOURTH 55

LOOKING OUT FOR THE LITTLE GUY 59

IN SEARCH OF
    POLITICAL PUNDITS 63

LONDON EYE, WASHINGTON I 67

CONNECTING THE DOTS 71

WORRYING MORE AND
    ENJOYING IT LESS 73

WHAT A DIFFERENCE A
    YEAR MAKES 77

ALLITERATION ONLY GOES SO FAR 81

AN AXIS OF MISOGYNY 85

WHOSE WELFARE IS IT, ANYWAY? 91

ON A WING AND A PRAYER 95

SECRETS AND THE SELLING OF
    AMERICA 99

A CALL FOR CLEAR THINKING 103

WHO'S ON FIRST WHEN IT COMES
    TO MORAL AUTHORITY? 107

THE REFUGE OF SCOUNDRELS 111

II

"AS A WOMAN, I HAVE NO NATION"

OUR MOTHERS, OUR DAUGHTERS,
OURSELVES: FACES IN
THE MIRROR 117

MOOD SWINGS AND MIDLIFE:
NEARLY GETTING TO NIRVANA 121

GOING TO THE RIVER............................. 127

A QUESTION OF CULTURE 131

INTO THE DIASPORA............................. 135

FINDING PEACE 137

WHAT YOU REALIZE ON THE ROAD 141

INSIDE MOMS 145

"TELL JAKE TO SLEEP ON THE ROOF" 149

BUDDHAS AND BURKAHS 153

TRAFFIC JAM 157

A JURY OF HER PEERS, ALMOST 161

REMEMBER THE WOMEN 169

WAITING FOR THE FAT LADY TO
SING 173

BOYS WILL BE BOYS, BUT FOR HOW LONG? 177

A MOVEMENT CONTINUES 181

MOTHERS AND MANAGERS:
   WORKING IT OUT 185

MARTYR MOMS, MANLY MOTIVES:
   WOMEN AND
   THE GLOBAL ECONOMY 189

OUTING MEDEA 195

THE PAUSE THAT DOESN'T REFRESH 199

INTERNATIONAL
   WOMEN'S DAY, 2002 203

FINDING OUR VOICE IN THE VOID 207

THE FEMALE FACE OF
   PHILANTHROPY 211

COOKS, CRONES, AND CHRISTMAS 215

MOMMY, MAY I? 219

FAIR PLAY:
   GIVING WOMEN EQUAL TIME IN
   THE MEDIA 221

SACRIFICIAL SILENCE 225

ABOVE ALL, DO NO HARM 229

A WHISTLE-BLOWER

WHO GOT LUCKY 233

WHAT'S IN A NAME? 237

WOMEN'S MENTAL HEALTH CARE:
  FRAUGHT WITH PROBLEMS 241

MERGERS THAT MATTER 247

III

SEPTEMBER 11, 2001

SEPTEMBER 11, 2001 253

IT'S ONLY DEATH 255

TURNING TOWARD SHALOM 257

STEAK KNIVES JUST WON'T CUT IT 261

THE HOMELESS, HUNGRY, TEMPEST TOSSED .. 263

"THE STEEL STILL PIERCES
  MY HEART" 267

PROACTIVE PACIFISM:
  OXYMORON OR REALITY? 271

THE POLITICAL IS PERSONAL 275

THINK HYSTERICALLY,
  ACT NORMALLY 279

GIVING THANKS FOR
  SIGNIFICANT OTHERS 283

IV

REFLECTIONS

SPRING CLEANING 289

WHO CENSORS THE CENSORS? 293

COMMUNICATING CONSERVATION:
LESSONS FROM THE
DEVELOPING WORLD 297

HAPPY BIRTHDAY, FLORENCE 301

THE VIRTUAL RAGE OF
A CYBERSPACE AGE 305

COURTESIES AND CRUELTIES:
POSTCARDS FROM THE EDGE 311

FIFTH AVENUE RAMBLE 317

GLUTTONY IN THE GLOBAL VILLAGE:
CAN THIS CONSUMER BE SAVED? 321

A BLAST IN THE DARK 325

NIGHT LIGHT 329

COURTESY CALLS 333

BEYOND MILLENNIAL MIDNIGHT 335

BEAUTY, HISTORY, CULTURE:
WHEREFORE ART THOU? 339

TILL DEATH DO US PART 343

A BREATH OF FRESH AIR 347

WAITING FOR HEAVEN 351

HOHUM HOMOGENEITY 355

MARGINAL MATTERS 359

PHARMACY FOR DUMMIES 363

WHERE IS THE P IN PUBLIC RADIO? 367

SABBATICAL 371

ON VALENTINES DAY, A LITTLE
    GIVE-AND-TAKE 375

THE FUTURE IS NOW 377

ON BECOMING AN ELDER...................................... 381

NET GAINS 385

PROMISING TO LOVE, HONOR,
    AND STAY 389

FOR RACHEL AND DAVID,
AND THEIR GENERATION,
IN THE HOPE THAT THEY CAN MAKE
THE DIFFERENCE.

. . . a state of complete physical, mental and social
well-being . . .

Health for All by the Year 2000,
World Health Organization goal

Sanity is a cozy lie.

Susan Sontag

ACKNOWLEDGMENTS

Many of these essays first appeared in the *Brattleboro (VT) Reformer,* the *Times Argus (VT),* and the *Keene (NH) Sentinel.* Some have appeared in the *Christian Science Monitor.*

"Mood Swings and Midlife: Nearly Getting to Nirvana" first appeared in *The Leap Years: Women Reflect on Change, Loss, and Love* (Maier & Isom, eds.), Beacon Press, 1999.

I

BEATING THE BUSHES AND
OTHER POLITICAL ACTS

SEX, LIES, AND SANDBOX POLITICS

It's been a long time since my political dander has been up like this. Not since the Clarence Thomas debacle, America's sex thriller of yesteryear in which a now-Supreme Court justice convinced himself and many others that he had not behaved inappropriately (depends on what you mean by "Coke bottle," I guess), have I been so glued to the melodrama of daytime television. The recent debate in the House of Representatives over President Clinton's actions and verbal sparring was sort of like watching a remade film: *The Man in the Gray Flannel Suit Boards Titantic,* or something like that. The question is, who was steering the ship? And who were all those men in gray flannel suits with such a prurient interest in presidential private life?

Let me say right up front that I'm really furious with Bill Clinton. His insatiable appetites, his poor judgment when those appetites kick in, his obfuscation and word games, his betrayal of those who are loyal and loving towards him, his demeaning of the high office he holds have brought us to a low point in American history, not because what he did was so inhumanly low, in my liberal view, but because he has caused us to waste so much valuable time, to look so pathetic in the eyes of the world, to be reduced to the time in history when the Congress of the United States will be remembered for its prolonged bickering over whether the president understood the meaning of the term "sexual relations." I'm most angry at Mr. Clinton because his behavior has deflected us from the real and pressing issues of the day about which he too cares so much. I'm absolutely stunned by his stupidity and impulsiveness in the Lewinsky matter, and I resent heartily the position he has put me in at social events when the inevitable feminist-baiting question arises: "So, what do you have to say about Clinton now?"

Don't get me wrong here, I'm one of those card-carrying liberal Democrats who loves this huggy-bear guy we call Mr. President, even when he has acted childishly and disappointed me beyond measure. I still think that when he is evaluated on the basis of those issues that legitimately belong in public discourse—domestic policy, foreign affairs, the economy, civil rights—he has established a record that any self-respecting Democrat can be proud of. But even people like me would have to admit, I think, that William Jefferson Clinton is the walking personification of that new adage, "Testosterone causes brain damage."

I'm equally furious at some members of the House subcommittee who seem to embody the observation that "absolute power corrupts absolutely." In this case, it seems to me that what has been corrupted, or at least co-opted, is certain members' ability to think beyond party politics and "gotcha" games. I am as astounded as I am frightened by the unwillingness of some members of the House to listen and truly hear, to rise above the rhetorical fray into cogent analysis and intelligent dialogue, to demonstrate to the American public that they have the intellect to decide well and wisely matters powerful enough to force upon us a constitutional crisis. The self-righteous indignation and stubborn staking of position recently exhibited by some of our elected officials should worry all of us who strive for truth and fairness, even in the political arena. And on a far more mundane level, let us ask ourselves this question: Who among Clinton's accusers would have been willing to stand up and volunteer to the world that *they'd* had repeated indiscretions, especially with a post-teenybopper suffering from delusions of grandeur and a surplus of female hormones (and, as it turned out, a really, really bad "friend")?

Then there's Ken Starr, whose fundamental (a deliberate word) dishonesty brings him perilously close to the legal brink. Here is a man who, it seems, puts his own political agenda first, who is willing to allow his personal vendetta to rise above the national interest if not the law itself, who is willing to use whatever machinations it takes to bring down a president because of philosophical and political differences. One is reminded of that most poignant of questions from the McCarthy days: "Have you no decency, Sir?" And of a certain congresswoman's characterization of her colleagues on Capitol Hill not so many years ago. "They are all," she said then, "just neanderthals in three-piece suits."

So who and where are the good guys in this case? They are everywhere. They are Everyman and Everywoman, in the mythical sense, who symbolize all those Americans who made their feelings clear on this matter from the start, who said, in one way or another, "For goodness sake (literally), let us be done with this obsession about bordello behavior and this cheapening of American history. Let us move on with the business of governance." From the very beginning, a majority of the American people have demonstrated the sense and sound judgment to differentiate between the private and the public, the personal and the political, the prurient and the precious.

Would that our politicians, and our president, had the same good sense and judgement. Then maybe we could all, at long last, return to those days when we prided ourselves on decent motives, honest and intelligent leadership, and entertaining nighttime television.

BEGGING YOUR PARDON

In light of President Clinton's eleventh hour pardon of Marc Rich, a fugitive from justice for tax evasion whose wife just happens to have donated over a million dollars to the Democratic Party, I'd like to introduce you to a friend of mine.

Teresa Christine Paulinkonis, TC to her friends, is an amazing woman. She reads voraciously, writes copious articles and letters, conducts workshops on domestic violence, looks after her mother, maintains many friendships, advocates for political prisoners, takes classes, and counts her blessings every day. What makes this amazing is that TC does it all from the largest women's prison in the U.S., where she will spend the rest of her life unless paroled.

TC has been in jail for 12 years. So has her mother. When she was 26, Teresa finally tried to stop the stepfather who had been sexually abusing her since she was 7. She struck him with a piece of metal while he was trying to rape her. He died from the blow. Her mother was nowhere near the scene. Still, the jury, which couldn't decide which one of them had done it, put them both away for 25 to life. Until that happened, TC's mother never knew that, like herself, her daughter was being sexually assaulted by the man she had married. Such is the nature of guilt among the abused.

During their trial, no psychological testing was ever conducted. Neither TC nor her mom were put on the stand. No one ever asked them during court proceedings if there had been abuse of any kind. They were convicted on the testimony of one person called by the state. And if the California Board of Prison Terms, fueled by a governor notorious for blocking paroles, chooses to deny them theirs in five years time, there is a good chance they will live out the rest of their lives in prison.

President Clinton's twilight pardons, while a good thing in many instances, must make TC and the dozens of other women incarcerated for self-defense sad if not outraged. Why, for example, should Dan Rostenkowski, a former congressman convicted of abuse of office, be pardoned? Convicted only four years ago, he spent a total of 451 days in a minimum-security prison and a halfway house. Hardly a lockdown facility with 7,000 inmates like TC's. Then there was Archie Schaffer, an Arkansas executive who got himself tangled up in the scandal involving Clinton's agriculture secretary, and Rick Hendrick, a NASCAR team owner who was sentenced for bribery and mail fraud. A political operative from New Hampshire who served as a Clinton delegate at the 1992 Democratic convention and former Missouri House Speaker Bob Griffin also got off.

Not everyone among the 62 people pardoned so far has been rich and famous. Kemba Smith and Dorothy Gaines were ordinary women who got involved with the wrong guys and ended up with severe prison terms for standing by their drug-dealing men (both of whose sentences were less severe than their girlfriends'). Nevertheless, it does begin to appear that clemency is for those with connections in high places.

My friend TC committed a terrible if inadvertent crime. She killed a man, and she has been willing to pay a debt. But she has spent 12 years in prison and presents no threat to society. Indeed, she has much to offer her peers and the community at large. Yet, without parole or a pardon, she will never be "outside" again. All that she might have contributed to society will remain locked away forever.

Dan Rostenkowski, on hearing his good news, said he was "appreciative." He vowed to go on with his life, teaching, writing, and giving "advice and counsel to people that need counseling with respect to government." Surely TC, and women like her, deserves the same chance. Their advice and counsel, unlike the former congressman's, could very well save someone's life.

SAY WHAT?

There was a time when I had difficulty explaining what an oxymoron was to my students. The best example I could come up with was "fresh from the tennis court." Nowadays, however, I find that examples abound. Take, for example, a compassionate conservative promising the global village virtual reality. To carry the concept further, consider a world conference of religious leaders discussing peace to which the Dalai Lama is denied entry because the United Nations, in all its wisdom, does not want to offend China. Now, I've been told never to discuss religion or politics at polite social gatherings, but the notion of a political religious forum or, for that matter, a religious political forum, which means every UN conference disrupted by the Holy See, is kind of ridiculous.

Here's another example of how we've come to accept as natural "a combination of contradictory or incongruous words" or ideas: I recently received a letter from a pen pal in Portugal that had a sticker on it reading, "Love your neighbor as yourself (Matthew 22:39)." This caused me to smile and scratch my head, because my friend and I have been having a transatlantic debate about civil union or, more broadly, about homosexuality. My friend, who is a devout

Christian, a mature woman, and, for the most part, a very sensible, kind human being, thinks that homosexuals are "abnormal." She would like them to be tolerated with kindness, much as you would any other nonthreatening "deviant." Some of her best friends are gay, she tells me, and she welcomes them into her neighborhood; she just doesn't want them to be fully legitimized in the eyes of the church or state. She does not seem to think that her position is in the least ironic, or that her stationery stickers are a strange and humorous metaphor for the oxymorons of 21st century life that seem to be enveloping us daily.

Included among such dichotomous realities are liberal thinkers who espouse inclusion and then exclude those with dissimilar viewpoints, organizations that fire women seeking to impose strict sexual harassment policies, and political administrations campaigning for better health care for all children when their own welfare programs resulted in 14 million of them losing clinic access.

I realize, of course, that it's stretching the point to call these examples the oxymorons of our time. Nevertheless, you'd have to concede they are rather moronic. More importantly, however, such incongruities remind us how prevalent and dangerous such double-speak can be. In an age of tag lines and sound bites, of negative advertising and careless character assessments, they tell us that we must listen carefully to what is being said and consider who is saying it. They remind us that doing a little homework can go a long way toward getting to the heart of matters. And perhaps most urgently, these examples serve to warn us that a glib tongue, no matter whose mouth it's attached to, is no substitute for substance, good sense, and civility in an age when such commodities seem to be in painfully short supply.

UP IN ARMS

So yet again we suffer the tragedy of children killing children. The perversion of school shootings. The ruined lives of teenagers poised on the cusp of an adult future that might have been healthy and productive after all. The sight of shackled kids in prison garb, heads down, shoved into cop cars. Weeping students giving eulogies. And in light of the most recent shootings, there is more talk of what makes children so unhappy and violent, of whether metal detectors are appropriate for schools, of parental responsibility. But amid all that chatter in print and over the airwaves, where is the public policy debate? Where is the issue of gun control? Where is adult sanity?

The statistics about gun violence in America are startling. Every day, more than 80 Americans—12 of them children— die from guns. In 1997 alone, more than 4,000 children under the age of 19 were killed by gunfire; that's one every two hours. More than 600 of these children were under the age of 15. American children are 12 times more likely to die from gunfire than children in 25 other industrialized countries combined, and gun homicide is the second leading cause of death for young people between the ages of 15 and 24. These are sobering facts.

But where is the issue of gun control?

For women like Carmen McCain, Veronica McQueen, and Congresswoman Carolyn McCarthy (D-NY), it is a bitter question. McCain's 16-year-old son, McQueen's 6-year-old daughter, and McCarthy's husband all lost their lives to gun violence. So did Abraham Lincoln, Martin Luther King, John and Bobby Kennedy. What will it take to put an end to this madness?

In 1999, at the Million Mom March on Washington, DC, aimed at stopping gun violence, three quarters of a million people showed up to let Congress know that "Twelve Kids a Day [Are] Too Many." Speakers asked, "Are we proud of a Congress which pontificates to us on morality and does nothing about gun control?" Angry, frightened mothers pleaded, "We are here to protect our children!" Many of those children carried pictures of lost playmates.

Yet a year and now several shootings later, where is the issue of gun control?

Let us be clear about what advocates of gun control want. We want a law requiring that all gun owners be licensed and registered. We want gun safety locks to be standard. We want mandatory safety training for gun owners. Why? Because current gun laws in America do little to limit gun sales or distribution. Existing weak gun laws are largely unenforceable because there is no national system to register handguns, track their movement into illegal markets, or hold accountable the people who sell or use weapons in a criminal or negligent manner. State laws tend to be inconsistent and contradictory, and avoiding a state law can be as simple as driving a few hours away to buy or sell a gun in another jurisdiction. Licensing and registering guns would be the same as licensing drivers and registering cars. It's that simple.

Still, the NRA triumphs. Gun enthusiasts hurl non-sequiturs, ("Guns don't kill people. People do.") Congress avoids the issue. And kids die in school. I'd say that on behalf of those kids, we grown-ups are all under the gun. So where is the issue of gun control?

CONSERVATIVE OR MEAN-SPIRITED?
THE FIRST *100+* DAYS

It's one thing to be conservative. It's quite another to be mean-spirited. And it's dangerous to be both.

There are several ways to view "conservative," so I won't try that one, but how's this for "mean-spirited"? Mean-spirited is when the president of the United States won't invite a state senator, who happens to serve on a committee dealing with education, to a ceremony honoring a teacher from his own home state. Mean-spirited is when the Senate majority leader (in this case Trent Lott) fires the congressional parliamentarian because he doesn't like his interpretation of parliamentary procedures. Mean-spirited is when, during the first 100 days of holding office, your rhetoric and reality part ways and you repeal a series of policies and programs designed to improve the health and welfare of the most vulnerable people you purport to serve, which usually means the poor, the female, and the young.

A recent report issued by the watchdog group "W Is Not

for Women" provides some alarming facts about the first 100 days of the Bush administration:

For a start, women are in big trouble economically. After years of progress toward parity, the economic gains women have made are quickly being eroded. The fact is that the president's tax plan provides very little relief in real terms for the average working woman, for low-income single mothers, or for the majority of elderly women. About 24 million children are adversely affected as well. For example, Mr. Bush's budget cuts the Equal Employment Opportunity Commission, vital to women's equality in the workplace, by $9 million below the level needed just to maintain current services. While women account for 60 percent of Social Security benefits, the president's budget seriously shortens the fund's solvency, thereby threatening the future of millions of American women. Women who earn $26,000, the median income for females in this country, will get about $200 in tax cuts, unlike those in the top 1 percent income bracket, who will realize over $50,000 in tax relief. About 36 percent of all single mothers and their families will receive no tax benefit from the Bush plan, nor will the nearly 1.5 million elderly women living alone in poverty with incomes below $7,450. "Women will feel the sting," as one advocate says.

In terms of health, women and children have suffered serious setbacks. In just a few short months, Messrs. Bush, Cheney, et al. have managed to reverse years of progress in the effort to improve the health status of the most vulnerable. Because women and children constitute the vast majority of the uninsured in this country (60 percent, or 25.2 million), cuts to programs aimed at increasing access and quality of care directly harm millions of them. It should have been taken as a serious signal when the administration slammed shut the doors of the Office for Women's Initiatives and Outreach, when it launched a review of the already FDA-approved RU486, and when it reinstituted the "global gag rule" banning federal funding to international organizations that even mention abortion as an option.

Here are just a few of the chilling facts related to health care cuts: The Centers for Disease Control and Prevention (CDC) Breast and Cervical Cancer Screening Activities, a vital screening source for low-income women, is slated for a 4 percent reduction in its budget. (Since it was established in 1990, this program alone has diagnosed over 5,800 breast cancers, 31,000 cervical lesions, and 500 cervical cancers.) HIV/AIDS treatment funds are to be frozen at this year's levels, despite inflation and the high cost of drugs. Although new infectious diseases continue to rise, CDC funds for tracking and fighting outbreaks and epidemics will lose $125.5 million, a dramatic 48 percent drop. Mental health and rural health care will also be cut.

Of course it's no secret that environmental safety and health are no longer a priority. Clean air and clean water don't seem to matter. The Bush administration's broken promise to curb carbon dioxide emissions was a clear signal that global warming—induced droughts, floods, storms, and diseases are not a concern for this president. Neither is the fact that, according to the National Academy of Sciences, arsenic in drinking water causes bladder, lung, and skin cancer and may cause kidney and liver cancer as well. (It can also cause birth defects and reproductive and other problems.) Cherished national monuments are now proposed sites for oil drilling, and nuclear power is decidedly "in," even though no one has a clue how to rid the earth of the massive amounts of plutonium that would result from more nuclear power plants. In what is perhaps a grand example of understatement, Wesley Warren of the National Resources Defense Council noted that "the Bush blueprint for the environment is shortsighted and especially shortchanges our children."

One need only look at Mr. Bush's choices for attorney

general, secretary of health and human services, and secretary of the interior to realize the clear message he is sending:

The welfare of women, children, the poor, and the powerless are simply not a priority for this administration. The environment is expendable. Live for today. It's every man [sic] for himself.

Compassionate conservatism? Sounds just plain mean-spirited to me.

POLITICAL PERSUASION OR PERSONALITY DISORDER?

Right about now there are a few guys I'd really like to get my hands on. I'd start with James Baker, whose reaction to the Florida Supreme Court's decision to count certain ballots was stunning. "It's a bad day for democracy," Bush's best pal said. Excuse me? Isn't democracy about making sure people's right to vote is not impinged upon? How could anyone suggest that freedom resides in disenfranchising the electorate? One is reminded of Oscar Wilde's remark that "America is the only country that went from barbarism to decadence without civilization in between." I can't wait to hear Mr. Baker's final assessment in this contentious election. I just hope he isn't wearing a brown shirt when he steps up to the podium.

Then there's Ralph Nader, without whose ego this whole mess might never have darkened democracy's doors. I've always thought of Mr. Nader as a decent fellow with brains. Surely, I thought, at the eleventh hour he'll step in to prevent something like this from happening. But no, true to his testosterone, good ole Ralph joined his machismo buddies in the political locker room. Never let it be said that sanity prevailed when an American election was at stake.

Actually, I think Nader may have done us a favor, inadvertently. The chaos resulting from his egomaniacal attempts to woo undecided and noncentrist voters has served to reveal something we all needed to know: Politics in the U.S. is just as down and dirty as it is anywhere else in the world. It is partisan to the max. And no one, not even "The Supremes," can be trusted to act in unbiased, neutral, or necessarily wise ways. This may not come as a surprise to a lot of folks; the truth is, it doesn't surprise me either. What does surprise—and frighten—me is the rhetoric surrounding the debate and the numbers of people who are all too ready, in the name of winning, to cast aside all that we are supposed to stand for. The demise of a democracy doesn't happen overnight. It is a slow, steady, slippery slope, and it begins with talk that is unreasoned, simplistic, selfish, reductionist. As Hitler wrote in *Mein Kampf*, "If you wish the sympathy of broad masses, then you must tell them the crudest and most stupid things."

There are some other guys whose recent political acts are also reprehensible and unreasoned. Take Benjamin Netanyahu and his buddy Ariel Sharon, whose selfish political aspirations have resulted in a Middle East crisis that threaten us all. Sharon's provocative visit to an Arab holy shrine was a calculated move on his and Netanyahu's part to discredit the already shaky Prime Minister Barak and his government, and things have played out exactly as Mr. Netanyahu and Mr. Sharon hoped they would. Barak has resigned, and Sharon can now run against him as head of the right-wing Likud party. The problem, among others, is that a lot of people, many of them children, have died as a result, and there is no end in sight to renewed hostilities. As a friend of mine living in Jordan puts it, "The peace talks are dominated by warriors whose lives have been spent justifying themselves, and meanwhile youngsters with no hope for the future are fighting a war of frustration while the U.S. does nothing but haggle over its next president."

That is a loaded quote any way you look at it. The world is indeed full of warriors so busy justifying their own raison d'etre that they cannot relate to the frustration and fear the rest of us feel. Whether it's haggling over the next president or healing ancient tribal rifts, neither simplistic, self-serving slogans nor calculated, prideful acts are going to take us forward into a safe and sane future. That goal, as elusive as it may seem, asks of each of us that we participate fully, deliberate well, and, perhaps above all else, never allow the personal to overtake the political. Poor Oscar Wilde learned this lesson too late. Adolf Hitler never learned it at all.

YOU CAN SAY THAT AGAIN!

Talk about your "subliminalated" messages! The night after George W. said that he didn't believe in them (following his notorious bureaucrats ad), I dreamed I was trying to beat a big black rat to death in my house. What would Mr. Bush say to that, I wonder?

At least he's right about one thing. As he said not long ago in Des Moines, "We cannot let terrorists and rogue nations hold this nation hostile." Des Moines was also the site of his statement on leadership: "A leadership is someone who brings people together." Now there's a politician for you if ever there was one. I was also glad to hear the Republican candidate assure farmers that they are not "secondary thoughts to a Bush administration. They will be in the forethought of our thinking," he promised in an interview with the Associated Press in August, and I'm sure that made all the farmers out there feel real good.

I'm also glad that W is taking the issue of capital punishment so seriously. Why, in June it was reported in the *Seattle Post-Intelligencer* that he had this to say: "I understand the emotionality of death penalty cases," following a particular case that had benefited from "full analyzation."

Mr. Bush also has strong feelings about states' rights. He is on record as of June that "states should have the right to enact reasonable laws and restrictions particularly to end the inhumane practice of ending a life that otherwise could live." He said that in Cleveland just after his profound statement about abortion. "If you're asking me as the president, would I understand reality, I do," he told MSNBC, reassuringly. It was also around that time, in Connecticut, that the Republican presidential candidate made his important remarks on the Social Security crisis. "There's not going to be enough people in the system to take advantage of people like me," he declared passionately. No wonder he told *U.S. News & World Report*, "I think anybody who doesn't think I'm smart enough to handle the job is underestimating."

Mr. Bush may well have been underestimated. After all, who else could have said with such conviction, "It's clearly a budget. It's got a lot of numbers in it," or, for that matter, "the past is over."

I like, too, how modest the man is about his family. "Laura and I really don't realize how bright our children is sometimes until we get an objective analysis," he told *Meet the Press* in April. Of course, education is big on his agenda. "Reading is the basics for all learning," he announced in Virginia.

Mr. Bush also takes a bipartisan stance when necessary. "It is not Reaganesque to support a tax plan that is Clinton in nature," he said in Los Angeles. That kind of statement requires real risk-taking, and as the man has noted, "It's evolutionary to be able to vote for yourself on the ballot." Perhaps that's why George W. "reject[s] any labeling [of him] because [he] happened to go to the university."

George W. Bush is a man who understands full well that you "can't take the high horse and then claim the low road," as he told reporters in South Carolina. I agree with him, too, that "we ought to make the pie higher." After all, "we need not only to eliminate the tollbooth to the middle class, we should knock down the tollbooth." Not only that, we need to ask ourselves, "will the highways on the Internet become more few?"

Mr. Bush is a man who knows "how hard it is for you to put food on your family," and his position on quotas is clear: "Quotas vulcanize society." He also recognizes that "this is still a dangerous world. It's a world of madmen and uncertainty and potential mential losses," as the *Financial Times* quoted only last January.

It's clear that George W. "will not stand for the subsidation of failure." He also has a firm foreign policy. He fully intends to "keep good relations with the Grecians," and he has determined without trepidation that the "Kosovians can move back in." So I think we all ought to take his political future seriously. As he himself has said, "If you're sick and tired of the politics of cynicism and polls and principles, come and join this campaign."

Source of quotes: Jacob Weisberg, chief political correspondent, Slate.

WHERE IS HEALTH CARE ON THE RADAR SCREEN?

Okay, so they mentioned the high cost of prescription drugs and bus trips to Canada. They uttered the word *Medicare,* and possibly even *access.* But where is health care, really, on the political agenda of either candidate?

At a time when 80-year-old women seek employment in order to pay for their medicine, when people take half their prescribed doses of medication to conserve, when a drug like Premarin costs 25 cents per tablet in Canada compared with $1 in the U.S., yes, it's time to talk about the pharmaceutical industry and the high cost of drugs in this country.

But where is HEALTH CARE on the radar screen? Why aren't we talking about the real issues: the privatization of health care and its ramifications, and our national resistance to universal coverage and equal access?

Ever since the Clinton administration's first-term debacle, both political parties have been running shy of condemning the disaster of HMOs and insurance-driven crises of care. Neither candidate from the two recognized parties will

45

articulate a cogent approach to sound health care delivery. Only Ralph Nader has been willing to take this bull by the horns, and he, quite literally, can't get a foot in the door.

Here are some of the realities of the day in terms of our public health: Overall health status among many groups such as the elderly, the marginally poor, and some children has declined. The incidence of certain cancers is higher than it's ever been, despite increased research funds, and the mortality rate remains the same or higher for many cancers, a fact that correlates with late diagnosis and restricted access to treatment as a result of poor insurance coverage. More women suffer from postpartum depression and decline to breast-feed their newborns since "drive-through deliveries" were introduced. Medication errors, often fatal, have increased because of personnel fatigue resulting from longer working hours to cover profit motivated human resource reductions. In a chilling three-part series for the *Chicago Tribune* published in September, Michael Berens wrote: "Overwhelmed and inadequately trained nurses kill and injure thousands of patients every year as hospitals sacrifice safety for an improved bottom line." Since 1995, Berens reports, more than 1,700 hospital patients have been accidentally killed and almost 10,000 others have been injured "from the actions or inactions of registered nurses across the country, who have seen their daily routine radically altered by cuts in staff and other belt-tightening in U.S. hospitals." This is not to condemn nurses. By and large, they are a competent brigade of caregivers. It is, however, a terrifying condemnation of what used to be considered the best health care delivery system in the world.

What happens when you put a human face to these numbers? You see 2-year-old Miguel Ferandez, who died from an overdose of sedatives administered by a newly graduated nurse who was left alone to perform a delicate medical procedure without appropriate training or supervision. Or you meet 61-year-old Shirley K., who suffered permanent brain damage because her pleas for help went unanswered. Or maybe you knew Deedra T., who at 38 bled to death after a hysterectomy because the one nurse for 20 patients just didn't have time to check on her.

We all have our own horror stories. One friend of mine was made to bring her dying husband home repeatedly until he broke his hip in a fall when she tried to move him from the bathroom to his bed. Ironically, once admitted to the hospital, he suffered an acute iatrogenic (hospital-induced) infection. Another friend ended up with emergency surgery because of a misdiagnosis that nearly cost her her life. And another nearly hemorrhaged to death waiting for someone from her HMO in Denver to tell her whether she could go to the emergency room in Washington. Enough!

It's time we put the politicians' feet to the fire on one of the major issues of our time. Whoever sits in the Oval Office cannot escape the reality of America's growing health care crisis; we ought to know what they intend to do about it. At election time, it's important that we all bring pressure to bear on this issue. And by the way, next time you need medical care or hospitalization, be sure to take an advocate along. Otherwise, profit driven mistakes could cost you even more than you bargained for.

THE POLITICAL MESSIAH

Don't get me wrong: I am among those who are thrilled by Al Gore's choice of running mate. Choosing Joe Lieberman shows *chutzpah,* which I admire, and should bring Gore *nochas,* and everyone knows Al could use some good luck right about now.

But I do wonder, as a political observer and as a Jew myself, what all the hype is about with respect to Mr. Lieberman's religion. Had Gore announced that Diane Feinstein would represent his chosen people, a Jewish woman, I could understand why the press might go wild over broken barriers. Had he selected a black to serve as vice president, or a Latino or Asian American, I would have gotten the point. But why is selecting a Jew headline news in the 21st century? Surely, when the Catholic Kennedy burst through the religious gates of American politics, we cleared this hurdle sufficiently to let it rest. So why is Lieberman being viewed as the Messiah?

And why are the media so caught up with the fact that Mr. Lieberman is a "practicing," "observant," "orthodox" Jew? What exactly do they mean by these ambiguous terms, how is an unenlightened electorate meant to interpret these adjectives, and why are such descriptors important? In my own mind and experience, a practicing, observant Jew attends religious services on Friday night and/or Saturday morning, wears a *yarmulke* and a *tallis,* or prayer shawl, during those services, observes the Sabbath, and perhaps keeps kosher. An orthodox Jew definitely keeps kosher and will begin his day with the prayer, "Thank God I was not born a woman." I like to think Joe Lieberman does not begin his day this way, and I'm sure that Al Gore does too, for obvious reasons. But you begin to see how confusing the Jewish lexicon might be for voters if not used accurately and consistently.

It also seems to me that while morality is laudable, important, timely, and American, Jews do not necessarily have a corner on that particular market. This in no way implies that Joe Lieberman isn't highly moral; I'm sure he is. But why does his Jewishness automatically imbue him with this mantle, and mantra?

There are those, of course, who will make a big *megillah* out of Jewish heritage this election, one way or the other. Word has it that neo-Nazi web sites are already flushed with the detritus of anti-Semitism. And there are those Jews who will no longer wonder which button to push in the voting booth; their button has already been pushed, all other issues having receded into the Diaspora. Neither polarity is appropriate or wise.

Leaving aside such extremist *mishagoss,* however, shouldn't we, in true Talmudic tradition, be asking ourselves why religion must be so politicized? In a country that prides itself on its plurality, shouldn't we simply be celebrating our diversity as part of the American fabric? As my Bubbe would have said, "*Oy,* from your mouth to God's ear! A *mitzvah!*"

IS THERE AN ARTIST IN THE HOUSE ... OR SENATE?

Sometimes the truth lies in unlikely places. You may search in earnest for it, but it remains illusive, until suddenly, there it is before you, in a metaphor, a symbol, an Aha! moment. Like watching a shell washed up from the sea reveal scary bits of netherworld debris, there are times when realizing what lies beneath the surface of what we see is surprising, off putting. Occasionally it is really important. This being an election year, the analogy has special significance for all of us.

This insight came to me when I read a review of Jane Alexander's memoir of her term as chair of the National Endowment for the Arts from 1993 to 1997, when she resigned after one term, her hair having turned absolutely white during her struggle to save the 25-year-old NEA. Alexander's reviewer begins his bleak essay thus: "The true cause for despair is her picture of the blind and deaf philistinism of American politics," (*New York Times Book Review*, July 30, 2000). He recounts the embattled former actress's growing disdain for a Republican Congress described as "nakedly hostile" toward the arts and "stubbornly intent on subverting the best interests of their constituents and their own beloved local arts institutions in favor of ideological purity and party loyalty." He quotes Alexander: "I felt despair over the level to which our federal government had sunk . . . . It is hard to know what a politician believes anymore because he is so beholden to the special interests of those who elected him. The system is so corrupt that it may not ever be fixed." Those are deeply troubling words from a woman undisputedly civilized, sensitive, and intelligent.

The first thing I ponder, of course, is this: How can a recalcitrant Congress be so obtuse about the role that art and culture play in the history of civilizations? On a more mundane level, have they never been into a museum to see the hoards of people queuing up, tickets in hand, to see a special exhibition, or families simply enjoying pictures on a Sunday afternoon? I expect not. (I lived in Washington, DC, for 30 years, and never once did I see a member of Congress or the cabinet at a museum or theater, with the exception of Janet Reno, who was often spotted in such places.)

But then larger questions loom. What else do the privileged members of Congress not know about American life? What do they not understand about our psyches, our priorities, our personal needs and preferences? And what do we not know about them? In the endless game of politics, how shall we ferret out the truth? How shall we know whom to trust with our heritage, and our future?

What should we make, for example, of the flip-flops of a party desperate to convey inclusion but with almost no black faces among its delegations? What should we think of a governor who stands proud of a record that includes being first in the nation for people living in poverty, first in air and water pollution, first in percentage of children without health insurance, first in executions, and fortieth to fiftieth in per capita spending for public education and health? How should we interpret a potential vice president's attempts to justify a voting record that includes casting 26 out of 27 votes against choice, votes against banning cop-killer bullets and plastic guns that evade airport security, against sanctioning clean air violators, against Head Start, against a Department of Education, against collecting hate-crime data, against Nelson Mandela's release, against the Equal Rights Amendment, against state funds for health insurance for the unemployed, against aid to low-income home buyers, and on and on? (And all this before the Democrats come out fighting—and pushing their own skeletons into the closet.) It is so deeply important that we act as thinking, knowledgeable voters—so deeply critical that we vote and vote smart! Because it's not about charisma in the Oval Office, or charmingly nuanced sound bites in strongly controlled TV debates, or "negative" campaign ads. It's about who has his finger on the button in a world of hot spots (the Balkans, India and Pakistan, the Middle East, to name a few), who will serve on the federal judiciary and the Supreme Court, who will be making policy that affects each and every one of us in all spheres of our lives for years to come.

If, as Keats said, "Beauty is truth, truth beauty—that is all ye know on earth and all ye need to know," then it's fairly simple. There is beauty in the face of a healthy, well nourished, well-educated child who is safe, and our representatives in Washington ought to know that. There will be truth in how they speak to us about everything from abortion to gun control to Social Security. Our job is to seek out that beauty, and to ensure that truth. If we do that now, we could save a lot more of us from having absolutely white hair four years from now.

RECALLING OUR FLAWS ON THE FOURTH

There's nothing like a Fourth of July celebration to make you rejoice in the old red, white, and blue. What could be more American than hot dogs, parades, picnics, and flags waving? And celebrate we should, for it's a wonderful (if still young) country, a democracy we can usually be proud of and glad to live in, inspired, my British husband reminds me, by England's Magna Carta of 1215.

Still, it may be just the right time to stop and reflect a bit on our moments of shame—those times in our brief history when we have not been so very noble or democratic, when in fact, we have behaved downright badly—for reflection on such times is at the heart of a democracy that strives to be the best it can be.

I'm not talking here about the heinously bad trip we've laid on Native Americans and blacks and the abuses we continue to heap on these peoples, even though such shameful abuses are rampant. I'm thinking more about moments and events in our past that are little known or quickly forgotten.

Last year at this time, for example, I was in Guatemala. While there, I learned of the terrible legacy of American politics in that Central American country during the Eisenhower administration. To protect our own timber interests, our government propped up a regime so oppressive and reactionary that its effects are still being felt, especially among the *campesino,* who tried to organize for the preservation of indigenous Mayan peoples. And Guatemala is only one example of how destructive selfishly motivated American intervention can be. (Name your right-wing dictator in Latin America, Africa, and elsewhere, and in all likelihood we propped him up.)

This year I happen to be reading the second volume of Blanche Wiesen Cook's extraordinary biography of Eleanor Roosevelt, which covers the years 1933 to 1938. I've learned some pretty disturbing things, like the fact that FDR absolutely refused to confront the racism that resulted in dozens of lynchings each year in the South. While ER was a great advocate on that front, she refused, as did her husband, to even mention the anti-Semitism in Germany that was sending its Jews to death camps. Keeping Huey Long and the boys down south happy, it seems, was a higher priority. Ironically, southern lynchings are back in the news, with the discovery of a list of people who were responsible for hanging Leo Frank in 1915 in Marietta, Georgia. Frank, a Jewish school superintendent and a Yankee, was accused of raping and killing a student. Sentenced to life in prison for what many claim was a setup, he was dragged from his cell one night and lynched. It is now known that the men who carried out this heinous deed were Marietta's leading citizens, including the judge who mandated his safekeeping.

Then there's Dred Scott, Sacco and Vanzetti, the Rosenbergs, Joe McCarthy, the Japanese internment, the War College, Kent State and Vietnam, Leonard Peltier and our other political prisoners, corporate greed, guns, capital punishment, the health care debacle, and more.

Past and present, as a nation, we surely have our moments

of shame. And while they shouldn't fall on our shoulders like rain on a parade, I think we would do well to remember some of those events as we look with pride upon our buntings and banners. At the very least, such remembrance will help keep us honest, perhaps even humble—not bad attributes at all to hope for, especially in an election year.

LOOKING OUT FOR THE LITTLE GUY

On the face of it, you wouldn't think a group of Cuban exiles in Florida trying to hang on to a little boy called Elian Gonzales had anything in common with the thousands of people who surged to Seattle and Washington, DC, in search of debt relief for developing countries. It took me a while to figure out the connection, even though I sensed something in the timing of these two events. Finally I got it: civil disobedience.

As others have pointed out during the demonstrations against them, The World Bank and the International Monetary Fund (IMF) have become symbols of something larger. People of all political persuasions, socioeconomic statuses, races, genders and ages didn't organize solely around Third World financial matters. They organized around something far more profound. I think at its most primal level they united out of fear, discontent, and, ultimately, rage. They coalesced because they felt invisible and increasingly powerless, the have-nots in a swelling world of haves. And it isn't just a money thing. It's about resources and decision-making and counting for something even if you don't happen to play Dow Jones or *Nasdaq* games.

It's also about ideology, and that's where the segue is to Elian. For better or worse, Elian's Cuban relatives in Miami really, really believe that Cuban communism will kill Elian, or at least his spirit and opportunity, if he is returned to his homeland. And they are prepared to take to the streets to be heard, just like the advocates who gathered in Seattle and Washington because they really, really believe that the World Trade Organization or the Bank or the IMF will hurt them, also the little guy. These are people who refuse to acquiesce without a fight in which, unlike children at the knees of adults, they are at least seen and heard. They are not about to let the faceless institutions of government or finance, more powerful than they can ever hope to be, "diss" them without some good old American activism.

And that, to my mind, is not such a bad thing. It reminds us of our roots, for one thing, and our fighting spirits, not to mention our identity. It says that our heritage is alive and kicking. More importantly, it underscores the meaning and the importance in a democratic society of civil disobedience (which we so admire when it occurs in places like Tiananmen Square). To quote Thoreau on the matter, for which he himself was jailed, "If we were left solely to the wordy wit of legislators [or bankers?] for our guidance, uncorrected by the seasoned experience and effectual complaints of the people, America would not long retain her rank among nations."

Thoreau was, of course, writing about heady matters of state—taxes, slavery, the entire fabric of a relatively new democracy. His deep commitment to individualism might be appropriately questioned in today's complex political world. Nonetheless, "is it not possible to take a step further toward recognizing and organizing the rights of man [*sic*]?" Is it not possible, without activists taking to the streets and demonstrating, for institutions to realize the complex human dimensions of global markets and free trade, and to attend to these issues in a way that benefits all of us? Is it not possible, without Cuban exiles disobeying the law, that a government agency with enormous power could exercise restraint in the name of treating a little boy like just a little boy?

Because that's really all he is: just a little guy who went with the tide and found himself on the shores of a strange and rather scary landscape—one that he had not created and that he deeply hoped would take notice that he was there.

IN SEARCH OF POLITICAL PUNDITS

Remember the good old days—before Corporate America owned the media—when newspapers still carried liberal political analysts and network TV journalists weren't afraid to ask the really tough questions? Often newscasters asked those hard questions a bit tongue in cheek, but they knew how to play the game brilliantly, and more importantly, they challenged would-be politicians in ways that mattered for those of us inclined to take the franchise seriously. I'm not talking here about Barbara Walters's special brand of voyeurism, or about the Larry King/Charlie Rose banter in which the hosts love cozying up to their political friends, with whom they are likely to play golf in the morning. What I miss is a little more of what Ted Koppel comes closest to: the hardcore, I-won't-let-you-get-away-with-that line of questioning. The questioning that tells us who the candidates really are, and what they truly stand for. I'm no political pundit, and much greater minds than mine have honed this skill, but here are some of the questions I'd love to have heard during the recently televised debates:

"What *exactly* did you mean, Mr. Bush, when you said 'I'd take him out,' referring to Saddam Hussein? . . . " "But, Sir, you didn't say 'take out the weapons,' you said "take him out.' What *precisely* would you do to 'take him out'?"

"Separation of church and state is a fundamental principle espoused by our Founding Fathers and upheld for over 200 years by our Supreme Court. Can each of you three gentlemen explain, then, your overt expressions of personal religious fervor as part of your political philosophy, and your commitment to have your private convictions carry over into secular life in our schools and other institutions?"

"Mr. Forbes, if Washington is so riddled with bureaucracy and what you seem to feel are enemies of the common people, why are you so eager to reside there and, *in specific terms*, what makes you think you can change that city's culture?" . . . "Can you be *specific* and name, say, five government agencies that you could actually alter ?" . . . "*Specifically*, how would you do that?"

"In a democracy, where free speech and an uncensored media are considered something of a Third Estate, Mr. Keyes, can you explain your uncontrolled animosity toward the press? Do you hold that all media, including the alternative and international presses, are the enemy, or is that opinion reserved for what is known as the American media establishment?"

"Mr. Bauer, Americans believe their right to privacy is sacrosanct. In light of that belief, if a referendum were held on privacy and reproductive choice, a majority of Americans would vote to uphold *Roe v. Wade*. What makes you think they would go along with your primary political agenda of overturning that landmark 1973 Supreme Court decision?"

"In 1997, I believe it was, Mr. Vice President, you declared something less than $500 in charitable donations on your income tax return. Can you explain that to the American people? And can you explain, in detail, your fund-raising practices, including those phone calls from the White

House and that visit to a Buddhist temple? And, Mr. Vice President, can you tell us how it was that while you were bringing tears to the eyes of Americans at the last Democratic National Convention with stories of your sister's tobacco-related death, you had, at the very same time, strong tobacco interests?"

"So, Mr. Bradley, *exactly* who would you cut out when those tough health care choices have to be made? And how would your Medicaid replacement program be funded, *exactly*?"

"Okay, Senator McCain, campaign finance reform is important, but what other domestic initiatives do you support? What foreign policy principles do you stand for?"

"And for all you gentlemen, what will it take in the way of personal catastrophe before you concede that universal health care is inevitable? Given the polarization of wealth and poverty in this country, and its inherent racism, how long do you think it will be before we undergo a serious social revolution, and what might the nature of that revolution be? How would you feel about gun control if your own child or grandchild were killed by a handgun? How will you handle the increasingly real threat of international terrorism? What is America's moral obligation when genocide occurs? Gentlemen? Are you still with us? Sirs?"

We still have a long way to go in the painful, pernicious, and often perjurious campaign leading up to the first election of the 21st century, and I, for one, would like to see some feisty journalism out there during the course of this history-making event. Not the sort of thing where a bunch of guys gang up on the sole woman reporter and shout louder than she is likely to, interpreting for us what they hold to be cardinal truths. I mean the kind of intelligent, honest, stimulating inquiry and discourse that used to mark truly provocative journalism. I'm talking about the kind of coverage that served audiences well in exercising their right to vote, that treated them like thinking adults, that wasn't afraid to take risks in the name of truth-telling. I'm remembering the greats, like Nancy Dickerson, Walter Cronkite, Charles Kuralt, and Ida B. Wells. And I'm hoping that kind of journalism is something we dare to revive, in everyone's best interest.

LONDON EYE,
WASHINGTON I

Having just returned from London, where I was when the Florida fiasco began, I can't help thinking about the similarities between the notorious London Eye and our recent election. London's newest attraction (outside the Tate Modern Museum) is the huge ferris wheel on the banks of the Thames that carries hundreds of people high above the majestic city every day since it went up as part of millennial celebrations. The dimensions of this monstrous wheel are difficult to comprehend; at its peak, it dwarfs everything around it, and on a clear day you can see all the way to the Millennial Dome and beyond. The workings of the Eye are vast, complex, awesome, and invisible. Webs of precise, technically developed units interact behind the scenes to ensure that the wheel stays on course. There is an emergency exit strategy. Those along for the ride can only hope for the best. Once locked inside the transparent bubble car, one is absolutely at the mercy of the wheel's machinery, which grinds slowly but steadily, carrying its human cargo to the peak, where they may feel exhilarated, unless they are fearful of the outcome. The Eye continues its denouement, depositing observers back where they started. The cycle feels interminable if you are given to anxieties of any sort, and for me, the journey felt absolutely precarious. At the apex, I had the distinct feeling that I'd had enough. Is it any wonder I see the Eye as a metaphor for the election?

Symbolism aside, my anxieties were not assuaged on the morning of November 8, 2000, when I woke at 6:00 A.M. (British time) to see who the next president would be. It will come as no surprise that when my husband woke me with a cup of tea and "it doesn't look good," I thought it was a bad dream. Hours later, when the extraordinary events had begun to unfold and we were glued to BBC, I continued my state of denial while observing the reactions of those around me. We had, of course, asked various people in our travels through France and Spain what they thought of the American election and the two candidates, and reactions were consistent. They can be summed up like this: No one could believe Bush had come so far, and nobody could figure out why Gore can't cut it. And everywhere, there was tremendous concern about American foreign policy and the future of diplomatic relations abroad.

But the reaction in England shifted on November 8 from the general to the specific. How, our friends and family wanted to know, could the media in America be so brazen (and so stupid)? How could a winner be declared before counting all the ballots? And what was the electoral college anyway? It's hard to explain all this in a country where only one source has the authority to declare a winner, where election results reside in public referenda, and where "campaign finance reform" has never been an issue because of stringent rules about who gets what from whom.

Beyond these vagaries, and much more important, was the reaction of people to American democracy at work. While some saw the demise of a superpower and the chaos of a corrupt nation, most were struck by watching the democratic process in action. As one commentator put it, "no one would ever tell us they'd found unopened ballot boxes. They'd have just been tossed in the bin!" Overall, it seems that American honesty, the commitment to true democracy, and the genius of the Founders in crafting a Constitution that covers all contingencies have impressed and reassured our neighbors on the other side of the Atlantic. I, for one, may not be altogether proud of our current product, but I can hold my head high when it comes to process. As I said upon disembarking from the London Eye, for better or worse, it's been quite a trip!

CONNECTING
THE DOTS

Remember the game you played as a kid where you connect the dots to see how many squares you can put your initial in? Well, I think it's time to revive that game—for politically powerful voting adults.

Voters in the United Kingdom made me think about this game recently when they overwhelmingly reelected Tony Blair and the Labour Party. (The British, it seems, have a voter turnout nearly double our own.) Hearing Mr. Blair's victory speech, one could see why. He understands, as do his constituents, how the dots of a sound economy are linked to those of social services for the less fortunate. He is able to connect the dots that join good health and a decent education to increased productivity, decreased hate and crime, and a level playing field. He can go beyond the rhetoric of tax cuts, the sound bites of growth and prosperity, the smirking self-assurance of myth and myopia. Don't get me wrong: Blair is no more perfect than any other politician. But he appears to get the point that feminists and other social activists have been making since the 1970s: The political really is personal.

So why is Mr. Bush's approval rating still relatively high?

Why can't Americans connect the dots? Here are just a few of the connections I wish Americans could make:

How can you be pro-life from conception to birth and then want to cut budgets for child care and development? For that matter, how can you be pro-life and pro-death penalty at the same time?

Why would you want to beef up a galactic defense system if you advocate nonintervention and preach isolationism? Exactly who is the enemy, anyway? How can threats of violence deter violence?

How can you diminish welfare without offering the basics (skills training; transportation; safe, affordable child care) in its place?

How can you claim the three *C* words—compassionate, conservative, Christian—and not take the word of Christ seriously: "Sell all thou hast and give to the poor; it is as easy for a rich man to enter the Kingdom of Heaven as for a camel to pass through the eye of a needle." Wasn't Jesus instructing the haves to share their wealth with the have-nots?

If you take away sex education and insurance coverage for contraception, how do you stop abortion, especially among poor women?

What *will* we do with all that plutonium? "Save [it] for future generations," as the rhetoric claims for the environment?

Was Trent Lott talking about "bipartisanship" when he declared "war on the Democratic Party?" And did the White House simply forget to invite Vermont Senator Jim Jeffords to the Rose Garden ceremony honoring a Vermont teacher just after Jeffords became an independent?

How can *anyone* be against gun control, campaign finance reform, and improved access to quality health care for all?

Seems like an awful lot of dots to connect to me, and unlike the Brits, we appear to have very few boxes with the letter *B* in them. Perhaps by our next election, we can do better.

Isn't it really as simple as child's play?

WORRYING MORE AND ENJOYING IT LESS

I've always been a worrier. I inherited the worry gene from my mother's side of the family, which also passed on the guilt gene. It's kind of a Jewish thing (although my Irish Catholic friends swear that it's an Irish Catholic thing). I have known countless people who never worried about anything at all until they met me. Now they can't stop worrying, which I reassure them is a good thing, because God knows, there is so much to worry about. I mean, just think about it: cancer, nuclear war, anthrax, Ebola and other hemorrhagic fevers, and that's just for starters.

I used to derive a perverse sense of security from worrying. My spurious logic went something like this: If I can conjure it up, it won't really happen because my thinking will preempt any and all lurking disaster. It was meant to work sort of like holding a cross in the face of the devil until he shrank into non-being.

Then along came a bushel of bad boys (and girls) in Washington, DC, and my preemptive theory went out the window. For one thing, who could possibly have imagined all the things there would be to worry about once George W. took over? And for another, these devils never look up from the sand in which their heads are buried. As if there were not already enough trouble brewing in the natural world, along comes an administration that still prefers to think that *Roe v. Wade* is simply two ways to cross the river, that animals are for wearing, and that fine art means having a room full of wigged patriarchal portraits staring at the rest of us peons.

Here are just a few of the things I've been worrying about since George took the oath and promised us bipartisan leadership:

How many (mostly) women will suffer repetitive motion injuries such as carpal tunnel syndrome before we remember that sound ergonomics makes for cost-saving health economics? Similarly, how many senior citizens will have to get sick before we realize that prescription drugs need to be affordable?

How much iodine does it take in the water to kill salmonella in the meat?

How long will it take us to stop being ridiculed all over the world for withdrawing from the long-negotiated and much-needed Kyoto Agreement?

Why are we building a humongous Star Wars military if we are going to isolate ourselves from the global community?

What will happen to the Chinese American scholars held hostage in China after the spy plane flight crew comes home?

How much oil must you drill in Alaska before the landscape changes and the wildlife disappears? How long will this take?

How will poor women and women in developing countries avoid abortion if they don't have access to family planning? And how will agencies that have received U.S. foreign assistance carry on without that assistance now that Mr. Bush has cut them off from all funding because he misunderstands, apparently, that our funds were always restricted to non-abortion-related services?

How will single moms with, say, two kids realize any benefit from the child tax credit if they earn less than $23,500 a year?

Why was the White House Office for Women's Initiatives and Outreach killed without anyone knowing about it, and why won't the president take any questions on the matter?

Why was FDA commissioner Jane Henney abruptly dismissed? Could it be that she approved mifepristone—or RU486 as it's commonly called—which is not only an effective abortifacient but also a highly effective drug therapy for many types of cancer?

I guess my biggest worry is this: Who are the real gatekeepers in such matters, and who is watching over them? Why did less than 40 percent of the electorate bother to vote in such critical times? If this much destruction has been wrought in just the first quarter of the first year, what lies ahead that none of us have dreamed of or thought to worry about?

I, for one, am feeling pretty guilty about my lack of foresight, and I'm absolutely terrified of what might be coming at us from whatever malevolent source. I think other people should start worrying too, regardless of their religious affiliation. Across the board, it seems the faith-based thing to do.

WHAT A DIFFERENCE A YEAR MAKES

It is more than a year since the debacle of last year's election, and according to the *New Yorker* ("Talk of the Town," December 24-31, 2001), it can now be claimed definitively that Al Gore really won after all. According to Hendrik Hertzberg, "there is no longer any doubt that more Florida voters intended to vote for Gore than for Bush. And we know, without question," he says, "that the losing candidate outpolled the winning one in the nation at large."

Whatever tenuous pleasure that may give many of us, Mr. Bush's first-year report card is a sobering reminder that in the event, a conservative Republican agenda has dominated the domestic scene. Without discrediting the Bush administration for any of its successes, real or perceived, especially in America's unexpected "war on terrorism," here are just a few disturbing realities of the past year.

The environment, for a start, is in big trouble. Largely through the regulatory process, according to the *New York Times*, Mr. Bush has allowed road building in national forests; reversed the phasing out of snowmobiles in national parks;

made it easier for mining companies to dig for gold, copper, and zinc on public lands; relaxed energy efficiency standards for air conditioners; barred the reintroduction of grizzly bears in the Northwest; and made it easier for developers to eliminate wastelands. His administration also approved the largest timber salvage operation in the nation's history, openly skirting the public appeals process (now in the courts). Let us not forget, either, that the administration pushed for oil drilling in a wildlife refuge in Alaska and rejected the international Kyoto treaty on global warming. Despite promises of research programs aimed at positively impacting the environment, relevant agencies have been told not to expect any additional resources.

Such doublespeak is all too common at 1600 Pennsylvania Avenue. While claiming to have "very aggressively" reached out to women and women's groups, the fact is that one of Mr. Bush's first acts was to eliminate the White House Office on Women's Initiatives and Outreach. Now he is threatening to shrink or do away with several federal offices charged with protecting women's interests and has stalled activity in others. For example, the 10 regional offices of the Labor Department's Women's Bureau are in jeopardy, as are panels that advise the military and the Department of Veterans Affairs on women's issues. Several offices involving women's health at the Food and Drug Administration (FDA) and the Centers for Disease Control and Prevention are at risk of consolidation. As one women's advocate put it, these worrying developments "undermine structures set up over years to ensure that American women can participate."

Women are among many Americans deeply concerned about numerous health issues, many of which go to the core of such fundamental rights as privacy and dignity. Abortion, for example, is clearly a privacy issue, as death and dying must remain rooted in dignity. In a recent poll, an amazing 67 percent of Americans claimed privacy as the most important political issue of our time. Yet, "General Attorney"

Ashcroft, as Jack Ohman of the *Portland Oregonian* dubbed him, persists in trying to invade our privacy and to deny our dignity. His interventions with respect to assisted suicide in Oregon fly in the face of medical ethics, states' rights, and a person's individual integrity and right to decide. Even the FDA has asserted that withholding "terminal sedation" in certain circumstances is inhumane. (The Center for Ethics and Professionalism defines terminal sedation as a "last resort clinical response to extreme, unrelieved physical suffering, the purpose of the medications is to render the patient unconscious to relieve suffering, not to intentionally end his or her life.") It would seem that a huge irony appears to be lost on Mr. Ashcroft and others of his political and religious persuasion: "Smaller government" has no place in the bedrooms, or the deathbeds, of the citizenry; a nation state that relishes capital punishment has no moral authority to legislate against abortion or, for that matter, stem cell research. Secrecy has no place in a democracy. Separation of church and state does.

In a recent review of his first year in office, Mr. Bush claimed that his administration was "upholding our constitutional liberties." Thus a further irony must be noted: the president failed to mention the military tribunals he decreed or the sweeping efforts of his administration to investigate some foreign nationals, efforts that include expanded government wiretapping and the monitoring of privileged communications between lawyers and their incarcerated clients. Looking ahead, the president hopes that Congress will grant him sweeping powers to negotiate trade agreements, allow federal money to be given to religious charities, and provide tax breaks and subsidies to energy companies. "We must look forward with determination and with resolve," the president claimed.

We must also look forward with caution and concern. Although foreign policy is hugely important and, in these troubling times, all-consuming, we must remember that vital issues on the domestic front also demand our attention.

Contemplating what transpired last year alone, the three years ahead of us could be overwhelmingly long and troubling. We must ensure that the "bold reforms" of this administration do not find us battered and bruised beyond repair when the next election rolls around in 2004. Among other things, our privacy and dignity depend on it.

ALLITERATION ONLY GOES SO FAR

When it comes to alliteration, "make no mistake about it," President Bush is truly an advocate. You'd have to admit, for example, that when used together, secrecy and national security do have a certain ring to them.

Mr. Bush is also big on the *C* word—*compassion*—which lends itself nicely to alliteration. Having chosen to run as the compassionate conservative, he is now advocating "compassionate coercion" in dealing with drug offenders. I'm not sure what that means exactly—maybe cops are supposed to kiss offenders on the forehead when they book them—butyou'd have to agree that the term does have an appealing *je ne sais quoi*.

Indeed, the president was quite compassionate about his own daughters' use of illegal substances, as he was when his niece, brother Jeb's daughter, was found to have some substance abuse issues. His compassion for the Christian Right, while guarded in public discourse, is well known. However, his compassion for friend Kenny Boy (a.k.a. Ken Lay) cooled a bit and grew cautious once the Enron scandal unfolded, which is understandable: You can't be too careful when it comes to pronouncements about compassion.

There are some *C* words that the president doesn't like very much. *Counting* gave him a bit of trouble back in November 2000. *Congress* always presents the possibility of problems. *Conservation* is definitely a *C* word to watch. So is *criticism,* as Tom Daschle found out when he bucked the big man on the budget. *Contributions* is another thorny one. The United Nations Population Fund is still waiting for its promised U.S. funds, and some states, including New Hampshire, haven't yet seen their federal home heating assistance. *Campaign finance* is another sticky wicket, although with Kenny Boy taking the Fifth, can reform be far behind?

On a more positive note, the term *climate change* does create far less cacophony than "global warming," and *Cheney* has a certain ring to it. *Laura* and *libraries* make a pleasant pair, as do *Barbara* and *Bush. George* and the *GOP* simply go together; you might even say they fit like a *glove. Kabul* and *Al Qaida* have a redundant ring, and *axis* and *evil,* while not alliterative, make perfect linguistic partners. The possibilities are positively endless in this game of gab.

However, the world of politics is more than a well-put polemic, and one can't be caustic and compassionate at the same time. As any parent knows, it's important to say what you mean and to mean what you say. So the president's posturing, whether around terrorism or taxes, environment or education, security or sanctions, is troubling. In both foreign and domestic policy, powerful rhetoric is one thing, but practical and reasoned action is another. The president, it seems to me, needs to watch his words, and his actions, carefully in the days ahead, because the world is watching, and it is worried. With a growing collective anxiety, people everywhere want to know if he will exercise care in the coming months, or if he will continue to take refuge in inflammatory and reckless language. Whichever way he goes, make no mistake about it: Language only leads you so far before the time comes to put your money where your mouth is, and as we all know, there's more to that than simple alliteration.

AN AXIS OF MISOGYNY

In an alarming deja vu reminiscent of the Reagan-Bush era, women's advocates are once again watching the guys in Power City. Current attempts by the Bush administration to downsize or eliminate federal offices dealing with women's issues, to withhold funding to the United Nations agency concerned with women's reproductive health, and to identify both embryo and fetus as "eligible for government health care" do not bode well.

A recent attempt to close 10 regional offices of the Department of Labor's Women's Bureau was thwarted when activists let the president know that such an event was unacceptable. The Women's Bureau, established in 1920, has played a key role in transforming women's experience in the workplace. The bureau helped establish the Fair Labor Standards Act in 1938, fought to establish the President's Commission on the Status of Women in the 1960s, and helped pass the 1963 Equal Pay Act. It advocates for opportunities for women in nontraditional occupations and was behind the Family and Medical Leave Act in 1993. When the Women's Bureau was established in 1920, there were 8 million women workers, about 20 percent of the workforce.

Today, 65 million American women are in the labor force or looking for work, and women fill nearly half the ranks of the employed. Nearly 7 million women belong to unions. According to the Working Women Department of the AFL-CIO, the largest union in the U.S., women today want what they did 80 years ago: paid sick and family leave, health insurance and control over work hours, and equal pay. Nevertheless, President Bush shut down the Women's Bureau equal pay program, as well as the White House Women's Initiatives Office, before trying to eliminate the Women's Bureau regional offices. "If the Bush administration believes that the federal government no longer needs to play a role in improving the lives of working women and their families, then the president truly doesn't understand the exhausting challenges so many women face," says Karen Nussbaum, director of Working Women/AFL-CIO. Sixty-nine members of the House of Representatives apparently agreed. After they sent a letter to the president complaining about the proposed closures, a Labor Department spokesperson declared, "The closure of the regional offices is completely off the table."

But the Women's Bureau offices aren't the only ones in jeopardy. Many women's advocates see the attempt to curtail the Women's Bureau as part of a pattern of defunding, understaffing, or altering government agencies and organizations working on women's issues. The Department of Defense Advisory Committee on Women in the Services, established 50 years ago, is said to be "under review." As one spokesperson put it, the department is seeking "new efficiencies" and "expects to emerge revitalized." The Department of Veterans Affairs Advisory Committee on Women Veterans is also in trouble.

The federal offices dealing with women's health in the Centers for Disease Control and Prevention and the Food and Drug Administration are said to be threatened with consolidation or downsizing as well. Even if Department of

Health and Human Services and similar National Institutes of Health offices remain in existence, they could be limited in their ability to perform. "The administration will find a way to batter these offices," fears Leslie Wolfe, director of the Center for Women's Policy Studies in Washington, DC. "Budgets can be cut, responsibilities limited, staff reduced. I have seen it before." Wolfe also worries that the administration's message will soon be that we don't really need "separate" women's offices, since our needs are allegedly being mainstreamed into departmental programs— a hard sell for women who know that conservative think tanks favor that ploy. Like others, Wolfe thinks that the Bush administration is becoming more subtle because "it is learning that a frontal assault such as eliminating offices will fail, or at least cause an outcry. But a more subdued approach such as reducing resources and responsibilities is likely to succeed because it will take place under the radar screen."

Karen Nussbaum agrees. "The administration thought it could cut back on the welfare of women without anyone noticing. But there was a hue and cry. So they are floating trial balloons to see how far they can go." Despite a good deal of posturing to make themselves attractive to women voters, Nussbaum says, it's really an "insider's game." Using what she calls a "Reagan template," the administration will cut budgets, and only those privy to information about resource allocation will realize what is actually going on. For many observers, such machinations are just the tip of the iceberg. That's why they are racing to cast the women's agenda in larger terms and to educate voters for the midterm and 2004 elections.

The administration's attack on women is not confined to the U.S. A fight now looms over the congressional fiscal-year 2002 foreign operations appropriation for the United Nations Population Fund (UNFPA). Mr. Bush is threatening to hold back at least some of the $34 million promised to UNFPA. Both House and Senate members, Republicans and

Democrats alike, are warning the White House that "there will be consequences" if the full allocation is not released.

Antiabortion rights lawmakers, led by Republican Representative Christopher Smith of New Jersey, are urging the president to withhold all money from UNFPA, charging that, among other things, it supports coercive family planning policies in China. Mr. Smith couldn't be more wrong. UNFPA negotiated carefully with China before agreeing to work there, and it works only in 32 counties where the government has lifted its controversial "one child per family" policy. UNFPA's emphasis wherever it works is on meeting basic health needs as a way to alleviate poverty which fosters instability and violence.

Thoraya Obaid, executive director of UNFPA, has appealed to Washington lawmakers to honor the U.S. commitment, reminding them that the agency supports maternal health care, provides assisted deliveries by trained health workers, offers HIV/AIDS prevention education, and fights domestic violence and rape. She has pointed out that the State Department's own report on China found that UNFPA was "doing a good job trying to help China move from an administrative approach to a voluntary approach with their family planning program."

At least some Republicans get it. A letter to President Bush signed by eight of his party members in Congress urged full funding. Secretary of State Colin Powell has testified to Congress that UNFPA "provides critical population assistance to developing countries." And an independent research organization has concluded that "the loss of U.S. funding will have a devastating impact on UNFPA's efforts to save women's lives and provide family planning in more than 140 countries around the world. Experts estimate that $34 million in family planning funding is enough to prevent 2 million unwanted pregnancies, nearly 800,000 abortions, 4,700 maternal deaths, almost 60,000 maternal illnesses, and more than 77,000 infant and child deaths."

Those are impressive numbers. Impressive, too, is the White House's "deep commitment to address issues that are important to American women and women throughout the world."

So, what exactly are they waiting for?

WHOSE WELFARE
IS IT, ANYWAY?

For the second time in two years, Louise is "between assignments." She recently lost her job as a contract manager when her company was acquired in a merger. A 57-year-old single mother, Louise now faces the daunting task of finding work in the aftermath of September 11, which sent the already faltering U.S. economy into a nosedive.

Nearly all the women who worked for the same firm as Louise have been laid off. They were the support staff, payroll clerks, and administrative assistants—positions usually filled by women. According to the Women's Bureau of the Department of Labor, most employed women in the U.S. work as technicians, sales personnel, clerical and administrative support staff, cashiers, and teachers. Many of these "pink-collar" jobs are the first to be cut in times of recession. Even though women still earn less than 80 cents to the dollar when compared with men, resulting in women earning an estimated $144 per week less than men for comparable work, their income is important to families. For women-headed households, it is absolutely vital.

Economic recession always affects those on the bottom. Women are often last hired and first fired, so layoffs have a devastating effect on them. According to Ellen Bravo, do-director of 9to5, National Association of Working Women, women often don't get severance pay or unemployment benefits because they haven't been in the system long enough. Bravo is especially concerned about women involved in the welfare-to-work programs introduced by the Clinton administration. As food service workers, cleaning and maintenance personnel, hotel maids, and such, they are largely left out of economic stimulus plans, which seldom work to benefit the hardest hit—a fact not lost on those who vigorously oppose the Bush administration's recent $25 billion tax cut to big corporations.

It is deeply important that unemployment benefits extend to those most in need, which is often women who are forced to work two or even three jobs to make ends meet. "People don't realize how much women were left out of the boom times. We have no savings to fall back on," says one such woman. In addition to the hardships imposed on low-wage workers, women's unemployment is a disaster for children. Data suggest that the bottom third of wage earners have a higher percentage of family members with special health and educational needs. These mothers need more time, not less, with their children, yet they tend to have the least flexible jobs.

According to some experts, the good news is that the current economic crisis will force legislators to take a hard look at who is being left out and why. They will then have to come up with creative solutions to address the structure of low-wage jobs and the reality for low-income workers. Once and for all, those in power will be forced to acknowledge that these are essential work and family issues, not fringe issues that continually fall off the radar screen whenever there is a national crisis.

Leslie Wolfe, president of the Center for Women's Policy Studies in Washington, DC, says that the focus must be on women with the lowest incomes, which means taking a hard look at Temporary Assistance for Needy Families, (TANF), which replaced the former welfare plan known as Aid to Families with Dependent Children (AFDC). Instituted in 1996 under President Bill Clinton, TANF comes up for reauthorization shortly, and activists hope the debate will recognize that women are essential to the U.S. economy, as well as to the families who depend on them.

"Nothing in the past compares to TANF," Wolfe points out. "Before, there was always a safety net. There was no time limit with AFDC, and you could go back on it if you lost your job. Now, you can't get back on. There's no safety net." TANF gives women two years to move from welfare to work, with a maximum five-year lifetime limit on receiving assistance. This is particularly alarming because, several pre-disaster years ago, the national economy was projected to create only half as many new low-skill jobs as there were welfare recipients targeted to enter the labor market. One 1997 study pointed out that if the normal growth in the labor force were to be factored in, the ratio of job seekers to jobs nationally would be nearly three to one.

Advocates are working hard to push for postsecondary education benefits for women on welfare so that they can move into economic self-sufficiency in a meaningful way. It is unacceptable to urge people to get a college education but leaving out low-income women on welfare. That message suggests that poor women don't deserve the same as the middle class, when the reality is that the vast majority of women do get off welfare, get jobs, and pay taxes, while their kids move on to college. And despite myths to the contrary, they don't have a dozen kids just to collect welfare checks.

We need to realize that low-income women are not villains. They deserve the same support we give displaced steelworkers. Access to education, which means counting school as time off welfare, would make an enormous difference to them. Research supports this. For example, the average person who attends a two-year community college earns about 10 percent more than someone without any college education, even without completing an associate's degree. The average expected lifetime earnings for a graduate with an associate's degree is about $250,000 more than for an individual with only a high school diploma.

Empowering women through education has far-reaching benefits that go beyond the financial ones. Studies in several states have found that postsecondary education not only increases women's income, but also improves their self-esteem, and their children's educational ambitions and has a dramatic impact on their quality of life.

So far, legislators seem blind to this kind of potential progress as they continue to demonize the poor. As one advocate put it, "TANF is patriarchy in the guise of public welfare policy. We need to reframe the debate," she says. "We can't put these issues on hold. Poor women don't have that kind of time."

Louise doesn't have that kind of time either. "I will survive, but it won't be easy. I just have to ask myself, Can I live without it?" It's a question welfare women grapple with every day, and one the folks in Congress probably never need to ask themselves at all.

ON A WING AND A PRAYER

Perhaps America's hottest TV show, *West Wing*, should be renamed. Surely *Right Wing* would be more apt. Anyone who thinks the Christian Right isn't having its way with us should think again. And we should all be thinking about how an ultraconservative agenda is making its way into public policy.

Let's start with calling a fetus a human being under the guise of better prenatal care. There are plenty of health policy analysts who see right through that one. The president's suggestion that poor women would have better access to maternal and child health programs just won't fly. There is absolutely nothing in his proposal that isn't already offered to the target audience through Medicaid and the Child Health Insurance Program. The deficits in eligibility that render millions of children, born and unborn, from receiving fundamental health care would not be alleviated by the president's thinly veiled attempt to end a woman's right to reproductive privacy and choice.

Then there is the administration's push for marriage in the proposed welfare reform bill, which comes up for reauthorization soon. In the first instance, such an idea is preposterous if one considers current reality. White, middle-class values and lifestyles have precious little to do with other American cultures, especially those of the poor and marginalized. When poverty prevails, violence is rampant, and living on the edge is the norm, does Mr. Bush really think that one partner, two kids, and a puppy is a viable and realistic vision? It is probably worth noting that 40 percent of poor children already live in two-parent households, and that there is absolutely no empirical evidence to suggest that premarital counseling or marital classes increase successful relationships or reduce poverty. But more to the point, patriarchy and its accompanying conservative agenda have no place in public welfare policy. Rather, the welfare debate needs to be reframed within the context of real life, and with a full recognition of the myth and misogyny that surround it.

The issue of stem cell research provides another example of right-wing intrusions into the national psyche. Note that the White House has engaged the services of Dr. Leon R. Kass, bioethicist and author of the 1998 book *The Ethics of Human Cloning*. So far, so good. But look closer. Dr. Kass, a scholar at the ultraconservative American Enterprise Institute, has also contributed to books such as *The Neoconservative Imagination*. Perhaps that's why the president named him chairman of the new National Bioethics Commission, which has the mandate of being "the conscience of our country." Is this the person we want guiding this administration on all ethical matters that relate to biomedicine? I don't think so. In the 1970s Dr. Kass opposed unequivocally the now commonplace practice of in-vitro fertilization, inferring that it would destroy marriage and motherhood as we know it. Now he opposes any kind of stem cell research because it derives from human embryos (which, remember, the administration claims are human beings.) It's important to understand here that there are two kinds of human cloning—reproductive and therapeutic.

The latter is what we are concerned with, and for research and treatment purposes aimed at myriad diseases and disabilities, this type of cloning goes no further than a clump of cells with potentially a very high value, as it turns out, for people with such maladies as Parkinson's disease, paralysis, and Alzheimer's. The National Academy of Sciences gives such stem cell research its full support. But Mr. Bush opposes all cloning. I "just don't think it's right," he has said in justification of his position on the matter. Dr. Kass, perhaps in more erudite terms, agrees, based on what he has called "the wisdom of repugnance," a phrase that sounds ironically like an oxymoron to me. Writing about this linguistic morass in the *New Yorker,* Jerome Groopman noted that "the problem with this argument is that it is impervious to reason." He points out that there is, however, "a tactical advantage" to this point of view. "It enables the Bush administration to accommodate the religious right without openly embracing fundamentalism."

Such skirting of overt fundamentalism while inculcating the Religious Right into national policy is what this administration is all about, and it's high time the 80-something percent of folks who think Mr. Bush is doing a fine job thought about all this. Flagwaving in times of national stress and solidarity is one thing, but federal fundamentalism is quite another. Just ask any woman who has had the courage to leave a violent relationship, or any man who hopes that his Alzheimer's disease will be arrested before he forgets what the debate was all about in the first place.

SECRETS AND THE SELLING OF AMERICA

Secrecy and propaganda are proverbial partners in crime. It's too perfect: Don't let the American public, or the rest of the world, know what's really going on, create an image that seems irresistible, and presto! You are what people think you are.

The administration's recent brush with overt fascism in the form of the proposed Office of Strategic Influence, whose opponents included Secretary of Defense Rumsfeld as well as other weighty Republicans, was very dark. Public and international outcries have, it seems, put an end to gothic notions of planting fake stories in the foreign press. (Or have they? Who's to know now? In the words of a once popular TV show: Who do you trust?)

But what other bizarre machinations might be up the sleeves of our so-called leadership, when stooping to such tactics was not out of the realm of possibility? We know that the media are being tightly controlled, especially when it comes to the truth about the "war on terrorism." In an unprecedented event, Vice President Dick Cheney had to be sued in court by the General Accounting Office because he wouldn't reveal what went on between his office and a few fallen giants in the energy sector. The president is less than forthcoming on a variety of matters, simply, one assumes, because of his sheer inability to articulate his thoughts and plans in any depth.

Add to this ridiculous Mata Hari mind-set the fact that the White House has hired a Madison Avenue ad exec, for beaucoup bucks, to fabricate a desirable image of this administration that will fly both here and abroad, and you have the makings of an even more outrageous Marx brothers farce. Except that this scenario is not hilarious; it's dangerous. When a nation cannot tell the truth, and when it must invent itself—actually create itself in it's own idealized image—something is definitely out of whack.

This "addiction to fiction," as *New York Times* columnist Maureen Dowd dubbed it, has gone beyond the pale. The Pentagon, it seems, has been talking to some TV and movie producers, the kind who make such films as *Black Hawk Down, Top Gun,* and *Pearl Harbor,* about a TV series that will profile American soldiers abroad. Dan Rather, among others, is up in arms (no pun intended). According to Dowd, he is reported to have said, "I'm outraged about the Hollywoodization of the military. Somebody's got to question whether it's good to limit independent reporting on the battlefield and access of journalists to military personnel, and then conspire with Hollywood." I'm with you there, Dan. Bingo.

This whole atmosphere of secrecy, censorship, and media hype orchestrated by the military gives me the creeps. What is really going on here, literally and metaphorically? Who are we to believe, and what don't we know? American history is riddled with "lies, lies, and more damn lies," and when the truth is forced to finally emerge, the picture is usually not pretty. (Think of all the denial around My Lai, Gulf War Syndrome, toxic waste dumps, racists' exoneration, and more.)

Call me naive, but the best way I know of for making friends and influencing people is to tell the truth, be a good neighbor, put your money where your mouth is, and pull your own weight. (There's a reason for truisms.) It's so much easier, and more honorable, than standing on your head trying to pull the foot out of your mouth—a posture that is hardly photogenic, whether for movies or TV.

I suggest that the White House and the Pentagon ask their Hollywood friends to drag out some historical footage for viewing. Perhaps if they could see the difference between the posturing of some politicians and the prose of others, if they could revisit the way a young John Kennedy inspired America and Truman before him stopped the buck here, they might get a grip in time to put an end, once and for all, to the insane idea that fictionalized identity and fabricated warfare make a nation strong.

Senator Barbara Mikulski (D-MD) once observed that "leadership is creating a state of mind in others." I hardly think she had Madison Avenue in mind when she uttered those words. But perhaps the late Barbara Jordan of Texas said it best: "The stakes are too high for government to be a spectator sport." And if nothing else, that is surely the truth.

A CALL FOR CLEAR THINKING

As my third-grade teacher used to say, it's time to put on our thinking caps. The current climate of crisis around terrorism, the situation in the Middle East, the Catholic Church, and other domestic and international problems should not be an excuse for sloppy thinking, spurious associations, or loose language. Just as the drought has brought water to dangerously low levels, American intellectual inquiry seems to be lacking. We are, it seems to me, in need of replenishment. To my way of thinking, very little clarity is trickling through as the serious issues of our time are debated. Instead, the morass of simplistic, antiquated, and accusatory rhetoric we hear on a daily basis only fuels the fires of emotion, while precious little in the way of intelligent analysis informs public discourse or policy decisions. Let me offer just three examples.

First, pedophilia is not about homosexuality. Nor is it about celibacy. It is certainly not about allowing women into the priesthood. Pedophilia is, according to Webster, "a sexual perversion in which children are the preferred sexual

103

object." Healthy homosexuals are not perverted, and they do not prefer children as partners. Barring homosexuals from entering seminaries or other institutions of religious training is not a solution to the scandal now enveloping the church. It is completely spurious to argue that case. Nor is allowing priests to marry the issue, although I personally am in favor of clergy living like other normal human beings, especially if they are vested with marital counseling. And while I would go to the mat on the issue of women being ordained, that debate has so little relevancy to the crisis at hand that I still don't know how it has entered into the fray. What the church, and everyone who cares about its future, must grapple with now is the perversion—or perhaps the disease—that seems to be so prevalent among priests. We know very little about pedophilia. What are its causes, its physiology, its psychology? Why are so many priests seemingly prone? Do young men, for example, choose the priesthood hoping to escape their own proclivities? Where are those questions in the dialogue?

Second, it should be clear to everyone that Mr. Arafat, for all his failings and weaknesses, is not Osama bin Laden. Terrorism is a two-way street, and this is 2002, not 1950. When it comes to conversations and pontifications about the Middle East crisis an appalling lack of reason seems to have overtaken even the most seasoned of legislators and other leaders; it is in itself terrifying. When people of otherwise sound mind and sensitivity talk about terrorism as an Arab trait but call Israel's incursions self-defense, when they cannot relate to the hopelessness young adults feel and can see in their acts only orchestrated self-destruction, when Arafat is a villain and Sharon is a victim, what has happened to plain old good sense? Where is history, culture, psychology in the discussion? Where is human kindness?

Third, when it comes to the environment and energy, consumption is the problem, not limited resources. Environmentalists have been trying to drive home this simple lesson for years—to no avail, it seems. Environmental protection does not mean reduced resources, and oil is not the only source of energy. When will we get it? The president's recent Clean Skies Initiative is a farce, an insulting play on words. The fact is that it will lead to increased air pollution because it allows for more toxic levels of several pollutants. Fossil fuels (like celibacy and outdated political ideologies) may no longer serve a purpose, and tough decisions are called for in both the short and long term. That does not mean that we should check our brains at the door.

We have a great deal to think about these days. From barren landscapes to bloodied bodies to bringing the church into the 21st century, every issue of our time calls for clear, humane, intelligent thinking. We cannot afford to avert our eyes, jerk our knees, or babble banal non-sequiturs. Like my third-grade teacher said, now more than ever, it is time to put on our thinking caps. Otherwise we may all be held back in ways we never imagined.

WHO'S ON FIRST WHEN IT COMES TO MORAL AUTHORITY?

One of the latest in catchy phrases to be bandied about since the Middle East began to implode again is *moral authority.* Senator Joseph Lieberman, for example, invoked the term when he spoke to demonstrators supporting Israel in a march on Washington, and others have glibly followed suit.

The trouble is that talking about moral authority as if it were something exclusively yours immediately implies that "we" have it and "they" don't. It takes an important and difficult universal concept like *morality* and co-opts it, simplifies it, and plants an imprint of ownership on its face, much as cattle are branded on other parts of their anatomy. It reduces something so very important to the pedestrian level of assuming that God is on your side at the kickoff. It is also incredibly arrogant and culturally imperialistic.

I have always been really embarrassed (for God, I think) when sports teams or individual players pray for success before a ball game or, for that matter, when soldiers pray for success on the battlefield. Such trivialization of prayer truly disturbs me. I also wonder why we think our God is the only one listening? If Buddhists and Hindus and assorted animists are praying to their gods for success too, why should we assume that we have a corner on the prayer market? In sports terms, every team has honed its skills, strategies, and physical competencies—their equivalent authorities—so how can one team claim to be better than the other, beyond the winning of a game here and there?

Similarly, but of far greater significance, in a scenario as complex and historically laden as the Arab-Israeli conflict, how can we Americans be so outrageously egotistical as to claim anything remotely like moral authority?

If we think of morality as "conformity to ideas of right human conduct," as *Webster's* does, we can probably all agree, for instance, that the harming or killing of other human beings constitutes a heinous act, no matter who commits it. But moral authority is a much more difficult concept involving modes of conduct as well as opinions, decisions, and power. The double-barreled term carries with it connotations of control, domination, rules, and truisms. The question is: Who's?

The current take on the Mideast crisis by those in authority in this country, and by many hard-liners abroad, is hardly moral, in my opinion. Nor is it informed by a real grasp of all the historical, cultural, psychosocial, and economic ramifications inherent in the situation. Such an understanding is so crucial to any resolution of the problem that it is not only silly but downright alarming for anyone to suggest that we can impose a moral authority on anyone else. Never mind the history of our own amoral behavior in a country or two.

Once again, we are being subjected to, and largely swallowing, reductionist terminology in place of sound analysis, strategic thinking, and appropriate action. It's so much easier, after all, to take the rhetorical high road than to figure out how to end the need for trenches. Once again, we are witness to the oversimplification of pseudoleadership, and once again, America's penchant for cultural arrogance prevails.

In some playing fields, such behavior would be deemed a costly foul. But in the courts and diamonds of diplomacy, there doesn't seem to be much of a penalty for overstepping boundaries. So far, very few observers even appear to be keeping score.

THE REFUGE OF SCOUNDRELS

I once had a colleague whom I thought of as the Ethel Merman of women's health. An endocrinologist with a flair for colorful clothes, glittering jewelry, and a brash wit, Estelle Ramey's groundbreaking work proved that testosterone was a greater biological stressor than estrogen, thereby putting an end to the mythical "weaker vessel" and the argument that "biology is destiny." In the 1950s, when she conducted her research, Dr. Ramey took a lot of heat for her findings. But when confronted by male scientists who liked to make fun of her study results because they threatened the status quo, her standard reply became something of a trademark. Cheap shots, she told her audience, were the last refuge of scoundrels.

That phrase has always stayed with me, and it is with me now as I contemplate (yet again) the behavior of President Bush and his administration. It is my firm belief that Estelle Ramey, like me, would say that Messrs. Bush, Cheney, Rumsfeld, et al. have been, for reasons of political expediency, behaving exactly like scoundrels, and I offer the following three examples.

First, consider the administration's response to criticism that it did not act appropriately to prevent the events of September 11, in view of information about FBI memos and the like leaked to the press. I think we can all agree that alarming Americans over "almost certain" terrorism by issuing warnings rife with hyperbole about untimed, nonspecific, potential acts of violence is hardly responsible. In fact, it's thoroughly reprehensible if, as many have suggested, it was done to divert attention from the administration's failures pre 9-11. The hypothetical terrorism we are now being alerted to smacks of defensive posturing, and the emphasis for many of us in such hypotheses is on the hype. Mr. Cheney and others defend the administration's position now, and before September, by saying that in order for the government to act, threats must be "actionable." Surely it would have been actionable to alert the FAA and the airlines to possible disaster and to beef up security back in the fall, without terrifying travelers and the general public. It is actionable to ask what can be done to ensure America's safety, and to take prudent steps. And surely it is actionable to take these steps without putting the public into a panic. As Adam Gopnik (whom I am fond of quoting) said in the *New Yorker,* "Our leaders, seemingly, have abandoned the first and oldest principle of leadership—don't panic the troops and always lead from the front—and have replaced it with a new model: frighten everybody you can and dive into a secure bunker."

Then there is the entire Cuban mess. Quite simply, how could President Bush keep a straight face while admonishing Cuba to hold "free and fair elections"? Has he forgotten so soon the debacle of his own election, when the Supreme Court, in an astonishing feat, put him over the top? Does Mr. Bush even realize that, for better or worse, all Cubans receive at least a solid primary education and have universal access to health care, while his own party struggles with issues of equity around such basic human rights? One can only watch with awe as this administration diverts attention from its own lapses in good judgment and human kindness by focusing on, and indeed inflating, the shortfalls of a little country that poses absolutely no threat to America or to democracy.

Finally, in an unprecedented act of Monday morning quarterbacking and overkill, the Immigration and Naturalization Service recently turned away a pregnant woman married to an American when she tried to come home. The woman, a Canadian who has permanent resident status in the U.S., had forgotten to take her green card with her on a hasty visit to see her ill father. This is, of course, the same INS that granted visas to two dead terrorists.

Secrecy, invasions of privacy, and fabrication are all milestones on the slippery slope to a police state. They are also the last, best refuge of scoundrels. No one understood this better than Estelle Ramey, who would love, no doubt, to belt out a lesson or two to the boys in the chorus, now that Ethel Merman is no longer here to do it.

II

"AS A WOMAN, I HAVE NO NATION"

"As a woman, I have no nation. As a woman, I want no nation. As a woman, the world is my nation."

Virginia Woolf

OUR MOTHERS, OUR DAUGHTERS, OURSELVES: FACES IN THE MIRROR

"As is the mother, so is her daughter," according to Ezekiel. Or as social activist, prison reformer, and feminist nun Sister Elaine Rolet puts it in her inimitable Bronx accent, "You never know. One day you put your arm in your sleeve and out comes your mother's hand!" Such cloning brings a smile to the lips of mothers who know all along that their daughters are reinventing them in new incarnations. But for some daughters, including my own—who often finds my hand coming out of her sleeve—recognizing their mothers in their own personas can be a shock.

Several events have caused me to contemplate this phenomenon. First, I watched the old Holly Hunter-Anne Bancroft film *Home for the Holidays* in which the overdrawn mother figure is so upsetting to the free-spirited daughter that she can hardly bear to spend the Thanksgiving weekend at home. Then my friend Vicky, a university professor, began to notice how many of her women students were complaining about their mothers. "I used to be very sympathetic when I was younger," she shared with our women's group. "But now that my own kids are grown up and acting the same way, it really scares me. And makes me mad. We give and give and give, and then they grow up and can't do anything but complain!" Finally, my own daughter came home "between assignments." She was here for six weeks, and we had a great time together, talking, shopping, sharing. But she too wanted to make perfectly clear that there were certain things she was never going to do or say or be that are most definitely part of my own makeup. "God help me if I ever say that to my kids!" she would say. Or, "I am never going to do that!" Then she would roll her eyes or give me The Look, her hand on her hip in exactly the same posture I assume when I am adamant about something.

Where does it come from, this mother-angst? Why am I sometimes perceived to be so toxic that my daughter must declare her distance? Will it take having a daughter of her own before she understands how hurtful it is to see in her face or hear in her tone how much I have irritated her? Nothing can wound me faster or more deeply than my daughter's declarations of nonalignment.

It helps, of course, to recall my relationship to my own mother. I adored her for her endless capacity to love me, but I also found as I grew older that her choice of clothes was no longer so tasteful. Some of her habits became irritating or downright embarrassing. And I certainly didn't want to look like her when I was 40. It also helped me to know, as we do by midlife (and as Holly Hunter learned by film's end), that for all her failings and faux pas, I needed my mother desperately, I loved her dearly, I was absolutely lost without her. When she died, I was 50 and had a wonderful family of my own, but I felt positively orphaned.

Mothers can also soothe themselves by remembering that no one trains us for mothering. No one tells us how tired and frustrated we will become, or that there will be days when we will not like our own children very much. (My confessing this once helped a friend of mine resurface after a prolonged postpartum depression.) But we do the best we can anyway, and for the most part, that is very good indeed. God knows we try. We ache, we struggle, we worry ourselves sick, we forfeit and go without, we plod, all in hopes that we will do no harm—and that our daughters (and sons) will love us anyway. Usually, they do. My daughter writes wonderful and moving notes to me now that she is an adult, and our phone conversations are full of friendship, even though I can throw her into an "I'll-never-do-that-myself" fit in a New York minute.

But that wondering, that longing to be validated and confirmed in our mothering, is what makes our daughters' separation, their passion for individuality and self, their rejection, so painful at times. Do they remember, we wonder? Do they ever really know what we feel for them, what we have gone through for their sakes, that we would throw ourselves down upon the railroad tracks and die for them every single day of our lives?

Of course they do. And of course they don't. Why should they, until their time has come? Such parting of the personas is as natural, as timeless, as the flow of waters from their source, and the agonies that arise from it for us moms are equally predictable. But isn't that, after all, what we've raised them for, to successfully and with confidence be their own persons?

Ecclesiastes tells us, "For every thing there is a season." We can trust, I think, that when the season of our daughters' awakening to their mothers is upon them, "when they look into the mirror," as writer Faye Moskowitz says, "they [will] love what they see." And they will be gracious enough to tell us so, for we have, as our mothers before us, waited patiently and for so long. I believe this because of what my daughter wrote on my Mother's Day card the year she turned 24. "You are my favorite," she said, "even though I would never say it out loud. I love you. I do. I do."

For every thing a season. For every season, a face in the mirror.

MOOD SWINGS AND MIDLIFE: NEARLY GETTING TO NIRVANA

In the beginning there was bliss: long, languid, delicious mornings reading in my sunfilled bedroom, absolute quiet surrounding me with the gorgeous sound of stillness; nature walks; coffee and the paper in local cafes; deep conversations with my best friend in California. And only the slightest, occasional moments of angst. I didn't worry about these uncomfortable little intrusions until I noticed that my wee lie-ins were extending to midmorning and that I was feeling ever so slightly reclusive and depressed. When I began to have fantasies of becoming either a rabbi or an emergency room nurse in order to imagine a meaningful future, I knew I was in crisis and called the coast.

"I really think I'm going crazy."

"Been there," my best friend said. "Didn't like it."

She'd just been fired and had come through a messy

divorce, whereas I had slid, not altogether voluntarily, from increasingly part-time work to quasi-retirement.

We spend a lot of time, my friend and I, processing our depression, anxiety, and panic attacks as we contemplate how, as positive and powerful women, we are going to live the final third of our lives. I articulate my need for meaning, creativity, and connectedness. She tells me that's why she loves me. When I tell her I am feeling spiritually hungry, she confesses she has started Hebrew lessons so that she can be Bas Mitzvah when she turns 60. Through all the years of our friendship, we have validated each other in this way through rough waters, bruised psyches, and the jungles of modern life and mean workplaces. Ours is a rare and wonderful relationship, and without her, I doubt I'd have made it this far intact.

Here are some of the things I've shared with her.

First, it has hit me (as I've pointed out elsewhere) that, despite my years of activism on behalf of the world's women, I'm never going to be in Gloria Steinem's Rolodex. Bella Abzug is not going to ask for my help, and Betty Friedan is, in all likelihood, not inclined to quote me. Staunch feminist that I am, I must come to grips with the fact that, at best, in the world of feisty feminists, I'm second string. This is very painful because I lived in a city where power and prestige are everything, and while I don't necessarily aspire to high-stakes political positioning, I can't bear feeling marginal either. I would like to feel that I'm still part of the action. At the same time, I want out. This odd dichotomy must be somewhat like being involved in a dysfunctional or abusive relationship. The activist agenda is my seducer, even though I know that once it has its way with me, I will inevitably get hurt. Yet my transcendent self wants to move to a higher plane, to leave behind the banalities of the working life in order to get in touch with my spiritual essence, to live a life of meaning. Much of my lie-in time is consumed with this dilemma.

I also contemplate the wholesale marketing of postmenopausal zest (PMZ) during my transcontinental phone calls. This trend is, generally speaking, a good thing. For too long before this movement began, menopause was considered a disorder if not a fatal disease, and older women were written off as just so much de-gendered detritus. My concern is that the wholesale selling of a zestful second half assumes that I haven't been living that way in the first place, and that thought has a way of riddling me with a kind of nondescript guilt when I strive for the high road. My personal theory is that PMZ plays well to women who have been liberated from limited adult lives, whatever form that may have taken. But I, for one, am tired. Worn out, actually, by running to catch up in my 30s and 40s. Exhausted by starting organizations, fighting political battles, creeping my way to a graduate degree, juggling multiple roles, struggling to keep a sagging spirit intact. I no longer have the requisite energy to get very excited about too many issues anymore. I'd actually like the second half (or the final third) to be anything but a mind-bender. I'd like it to be easy, comfortable, and ever so slightly self-indulgent. So why is a good Jewish girl like me burdened with such an insatiable Protestant ethic embedded in my brain?

Along these lines, there's the issue of aging. All the hype about PMZ notwithstanding, I can't altogether buy into the power surge package. Yes, it's liberating to be post-50, but let's face it, there's also the firm-to-flab phenomenon, not to mention fatigue and the fatalism of our inevitable demise. I wonder all too often where my muscle tone, my stamina, and my libido have gone. In short, aging gives me the blahs big time. I get irritated by Lauren Hutton's radio commercials in which she coos, "I love my age! I wouldn't go back to being 21 for anything!" This from a woman who has never borne, birthed, schlepped, or nursed babies and who spends God knows how many hours every day with a personal trainer? Please!

But the larger issue as I search for midlife balance, tranquillity and purpose has to do with meaning and where one finds it.

When I was in my 20s, it seems to me, I wanted to know the meaning of life. In my 30s, I quested for meaningful work. By the time I entered my 40s, I was satisfied if I could simply figure out what things meant (in the cosmic sense, of course). But now that I've entered my 50s—the ultimate "mean," if not median—I find I'm oddly disinterested in much of what usually imbues a certain kind of activity with meaning. I'm increasingly de-invested. Lazy, perhaps. At any rate, I no longer seem driven. If I died tomorrow, I figure, I'd still have a pretty impressive obituary.

At the same time, because this seeming ennui is rather out of character for me, it has become a source of psychic conflict. My present struggle, if written as an equation, might look something like this:

$$A = \frac{P\text{-}M}{ML}$$

or, Angst = Personality minus Motivation over Modern Life.

One of my problems is I continually feel like I've "been there, done that," and there's a weird sort of deja vu quality to most events; my life seems to keep repeating itself. I long for something truly original to occur, for some Aha! experience, for new nuance. Instead, I am beginning to feel like people do when they say, "Y' know, if you live long enough, all faces start to look the same." Sometimes I think this is nothing more than the winter blues, or the summer doldrums. But no variation in temperature, humidity, or daylight seems to affect my lingering malaise.

There is an upside to this, of course. It's great not to be so driven or crazed with the quest for achievement. I like the fact that I'm finally learning the art of laid-back living. I really do smell the roses differently these days. But a little bit of motivation in moderation wouldn't hurt either.

So, am I having a mild mood swing, a true midlife crisis, a great growth spurt, or am I simply poised to plunge into the depths of despair? Perhaps I've stumbled onto something—the Great Transition, that spiritual awakening that comes of soulful solitude. Or maybe I just need a new cause, a new town.

While I make light here of my struggle for passage, my quest for renewed identity and newfound energy at midlife (plus) is really no laughing matter. I have had deep moments of pain and confusion, isolation and fear, as I experience the birth of a redirected self. Had I tried to write this piece before my most recent soul-cleansing California call, it might have read quite differently and been a solemn affair. But right now— this minute—having understood that I am not alone and that my quest is not a unique thing after all, I can lighten up, take my time, see the options as a gift. It is not always so. Sometimes, in place of those options, there is a terrifying void looming 30 years large ahead. When those dark moments seem more than I can possibly sort out, I try to remind myself that I am in the best of company. It is indeed a good thing, needing the creativity, the meaning, the connection to a wider world, and we women who seek it are not the crazies. We are, rather, the caretakers of souls—our own, and very often those of the people we love. It is good to examine our past lives now and again, to discard what is moldy and faded, to air the treasures in which there is still life, to add a few new pieces to our traveling repertoire. Deep down, I know this. Just as I know that the passage is worth the pain and that one day, as surely as I am sitting here writing this, I will find myself, at least for a time, in new and comfortable terrain.

Of course, no matter where I end up, there will always be a direct line to California. And at the end of the day, that, perhaps, is the most comforting thought of all.

GOING TO THE RIVER

Women are returning to the river. They are migrating to the source of life, just as they have always done, perhaps now with a new sense of urgency. They are gathering on shores both literal and metaphorical; they are finding each other, for nourishment, in gatherings large and small. The women are going to the river.

In one of development's great failed experiments, in a village in Latin America, the women went to the river. They went despite the huts with washing machines, an innovation that had been installed so that their labor might be lessened. They went to the river to wash their clothes because that is where the sisters were, and the sisters were community, a life-support system, recreation, respite. The river is where women gathered to learn, to speak truth in safety and affirmation, to laugh, to be heard, to be. Through the ages, in rural and in urban lands, in lean times and in times of plenty, in peace and in unrest, women have gone to the river—the source of life—to fetch water, to bathe, to wash, to commune.

Now, in our time, women are returning to the river. In symbolic gestures, in ceremonies, in all kinds of ways, they

127

are reaching out and finding each other. In a climate of massive disconnect, women are gathering together out of their hunger, their need for connectedness, their natural affinity for fun and creative community. It is an act of survival, a natural response. It is the quest for women's culture.

Mona Lake Jones understood this culture when she wrote her poem "A Room Full of Sisters," which begins with the lines: "A room full of sisters, like jewels in a crown, vanilla, cinnamon and dark chocolate brown." So does Melina Carnicelli, who, along with her colleagues, was inspired by Jones's poem to found Room Full of Sisters, an annual event in Auburn, New York, that has grown by leaps and bounds since it was started four years ago. A Room Full of Sisters, billed as "a celebration of all women," has diffused to other cities and towns in New York State and beyond. It has grown from a simple luncheon for several women to a day of events for several hundred in numerous venues around the country. Similarly, The Crone Connection, a small, women-owned enterprise "for women of wit and wisdom" over 50, was started in 1997 by two lifelong friends to bring together midlife and older women who are resurrecting in droves the notion of *crone*, the respected postmenopausal woman of prepatriarchal times. All over the country, and indeed, all over the world, women are reaching out, finding each other, connecting in both formal and informal ways. Whether for networking, personal growth, validation, or just plain fun, women are once again going to the river.

Some of this activity takes place on a grand scale. In 1985, for example, more than 14,000 women gathered in Nairobi, Kenya, for the United Nations Decade on Women conference. Flowing into the grounds of Nairobi University, they were a veritable river unto themselves. Ten years later, 40,000 women gathered in Beijing, China, to reflect on that decade and to ensure women's place in the world. In the interim, women's fora have taken place all over the globe. But not all women's connections are so colossal or so visible.

Some women simply have a walking group, a reading group, a writing group, a circle of friends who gather for meals. Some, through "the strength of weak ties," the networking that women are so good at, are finding each other for new friendships, especially important for those who have chosen to work at home rather than be co-opted by the largely male-driven model of corporate America. Going to the river also crosses all kinds of boundaries these days. It is intergenerational (my daughter comes home when she needs a fix, I'm thrilled to say) and it is beginning to jump the barriers of race, class, and ethnicity.

Its significance is also being recognized empirically. A landmark study carried out at the University of California Los Angeles in 2001 found that women responded to stress with "a cascade of brain chemicals" that cause us to make and maintain friendships with other women. This finding stands on its ear the male model of "fight or flight" when under stress. According to the researchers, when the hormone oxytocin is released as part of the stress response in a woman, she tends to her children and gathers with other women, which triggers more oxytocin to be released, which further counters stress and produces a calming effect. Estrogen enhances this phenomenon; testosterone reduces it. Such "tend and befriend" behavior may explain why women outlive men.

Just recently, I made two new friends, one on my own, and one through a mutual connection. Now the three of us are planning a walk in the woods, a lunch, or whatever together. I expect in the days to come, we will pool our contacts and hold a *femme soiree* of sorts. And it won't matter where the event takes place, because wherever it is, we will all be, figuratively speaking, at the river. Being there, cooling ourselves and drinking in its nourishment, is what keeps us all alive, and that is why we always find our way there.

No matter what, women will always know the shortest route to the river.

A QUESTION OF CULTURE

"How are we going to deal with diversity in the United States and what it means to be an American?" a noted anthropologist asked not long ago. "It's a great dilemma." The professor and some of his colleagues, it seems, want to be sure that American law will accommodate virtually any kind of practice—including female circumcision—in the name of tolerance for culture and tradition.

According to a *New York Times* article ("Testing the Limits of Tolerance as Cultures Mix," March 6, 1999), many theorists and academicians are worried that we will force immigrants into "compliance with the cultural and legal norms of American middle class life," and that "despite our pluralistic ideals, something . . . like a cultural un-American activities list seems to have begun circulating among . . . representatives . . . of mainstream culture."

The questions and concerns this group of cultural relativists raises are not unfounded, nor are the issues they are dealing with simple. While there are any number of norms and practices across cultures that most of us would agree are innocuous and even worthy of upholding, some of these norms and practices range from dubious to dangerous. For example, what is so wrong with head coverings in school? What harm is there in children nestling into bed with their parents? Are dress codes really an issue? However, when it comes to practices such as arranged marriage, polygamy, segregated gender roles, and corporal punishment, things get a bit stickier. Then there is dowry death, suttee, and female genital alteration. Isn't this the point at which, clearly, one has gone beyond diversity and entered the realm of destructive and deadly ritual?

If you have ever heard the stories of infibulated (circumcised) women, or heard the cries and screams of little girls undergoing the primitive cutting by razor or glass; if you have ever read the literature that does not leave the regions of the world where the practice is carried out (testimonies by girls and women who have seen their sisters, daughters, and mothers die from excruciating infection or complicated childbirth); if you have ever seen the practice captured on videotape, or observed the absence of genitalia on women who have been subjected to infibulation (removal of the clitoris and labia), you can have no doubt that "female genital mutilation" is not a practice to be defended in the name of culture and tradition. It seems ludicrous to imagine that any group of educated people would advocate for anything that comes close to fostering such practices in the United States.

There is one litmus test, it seems to me, that could be applied in the case of practices that involve altering one's person: Does it do harm, and is it being done with the full consent of the subject? The latter part of this criterion suggests, intentionally, that the subject must be adult enough to make such a decision. (Such a criterion would do much for the human rights of children. For example, child marriage and trafficking in children would no longer be viable.)

Urban Jonsson, who directs UNICEF in sub-Saharan Africa, has concluded that there is "a global moral minimum" advocated by Africans, Asians, and Western human rights activists. "There is a non-ethnocentric global morality," he says, "and scholars would be better occupied looking for it rather than denying it." Jonsson is upset by "the anthropological interest in mystifying what we have already demystified." He is not shy about labeling cultural relativists "partners of the tormentors."

To this perspective, add the concerns of Jessica Neuwirth, an international lawyer and director of the New York-based organization Equality Now. Neuwirth also asks why the practices that cultural relativists want to condone so often involve women: how they dress, what they own, where they go, how their bodies can be used. "Culture is male-patrolled in the way that it is created and transmitted. People who control culture tend to be the people in power . . . . People forget that inside every culture, there is a whole spectrum of ideas and values."

Neuwirth's reminder is important for the anthropology professor and his colleagues to note in light of their view that amputating women's genitalia is no more traumatic than male circumcision (ironically, this pronouncement came the very week that the American Pediatric Association declared the circumcising of little boys to be a low-value, high-pain event). The arrogance of such a claim (not to mention the misinformation) coming from a male of great advantage in a culture that has never condoned such cruelty is an affront of the highest order! I challenge him to witness the cutting off of the labia and clitoris of a 2-year-old little girl, to observe the painful, distended abdomen of a 15-year-old with retained menses, to imagine a woman subjected to forced penetration on her wedding night of the minuscule opening left to her, and then tell American lawmakers that they should accommodate such a practice.

At a conference on culture and progress taking place in the ivory towers of Harvard University's Center for International Affairs, I hope Mr. Jonsson and Ms. Neuwirth will be present to dialogue with the anthropology professor and his tradition-bound colleagues. Maybe, since it is unlikely that children and young women from Africa and Asia will be present to speak for themselves, they can show the professors a few pictures or run some videos so that reality is allowed to intrude upon relativism. And then, maybe, the professors will come to their collective, culture-bound senses. On behalf of the millions of girls who die or are maimed daily around the world in the name of tradition, we can only hope.

INTO THE DIASPORA

It is all too familiar: the bent bodies of women who have too little time to bake bread, the exhausted and frightened children, the terrified girls with tears in their eyes, the bewildered and bedraggled old men, the marking on the doors to be saved. Only this time, it is not the blood of a lamb but a red painted "S." The villain is not the Pharaoh in Egypt but a monstrous dictator called Milosevic. The firstborn sons will not be saved but savaged in this, the 20th century's continuing story of religious intolerance and oppression.

In 1999 (5760 on the Jewish calendar), the story of the exodus from Egypt that Jews have been telling at the Passover Seder for thousands of years is chilling and contemporary. It is also history as prologue. Who among us at the tables of the world celebrating our own liberation does not equate Kosovor with Kiev, Bosnia with biblical tales of persecution, Sarejevo with 16th century Spain, Croatia with the Crusades? Who can forget what we have seen in our own times of man's inhumanity to man from Jerusalem to Belfast, from Rwanda to Robbins Island?

The capacity for evil in human nature looms large to challenge our philosophical and religious notions of "soul."

Religion per se, meant to strengthen and enlighten us, in fact and deed destroys that very soul. Politics and power make aberrations of us all. Ethnicity, the very diversity we claim to celebrate and honor, divides and destroys whatever higher order we may claim. Is there no transcendence after all?

At this Seder, I dip the bitter herbs in salt water, remembering the tears of my ancestors who suffered as slaves millennia ago. But I weep new tears for those who suffer still, for the eternal "huddled masses yearning to be free." For them, the pilgrims of the new diaspora, there is no lantern raised and very little hope, it seems, that from their exodus we will learn anything at all.

FINDING PEACE

If the poet and humanist Muriel Rukeyser were alive today, what would she say about the current crisis in Kosovo? As an ardent pacifist who experienced the Spanish civil war firsthand and who lived, spiritually, close to World War II, what would her position be, and what response would she give to those who oppose the NATO bombing campaign but are unable to offer an alternative solution to meeting the evil of Slobodan Milosevic head-on. I wonder about this because of my own struggle for dialogue on the issue with my friends and acquaintances who are, understandably, against the destruction the allies wreak in the region but who, curiously, never seem to speak about the deep suffering of the thousands upon thousands of people wandering the refugee camps of Albania and Macedonia while trying to make sense of what was once their lives.

I have had e-mail conversations with my liberal friends in other parts of the world, cocktail conversations with German Jews who themselves escaped fascist atrocities in 1940s Germany, and heated conversations with new acquaintances, and for the most part, they argue against NATO's strategy in rhetoric rich with pacifism and fiery feeling for the suffering Serbs, but rife with gaps of emotion and logic when it comes to the ethnic Albanians doomed to the diaspora of our day.

What would Muriel Rukeyser, the woman who saw poetry as "usable truth," say? As one who was always alert to the terrors of war and repressive regimes (as writer Jane Cooper has pointed out) and as a woman with a passionate vision of what it could mean to be an American, how would Rukeyser speak to those who argue against action, believing as she did, profoundly, in relationships that dissolve boundaries and strive for one world in "peace that is not lack of war, but fierce and positive"?

Concerned with "outrage and possibility," with the problem of evil, with "finding the truth and power in diversity," Rukeyser would have seen the need for decisive action against the tyranny of what one Eastern European friend of mine has called "the last of the monstrous Communist dictatorships." Rukeyser was a woman who saw "the truths of conflicts and power over the land," who heard refugees "crying to us, their wounds, the young and the unborn," who knew "the crimes of those places: rape, arrogance killing the chance of life, the ignorant stoppage of youth, the poverty that invites every repressive force, the robbery of spirit, every kind of murder." A dedicated pacifist, in that she understood the ways in which war invades our spirits and enters deeply into our personal lives, she also recognized that Americans are "a people tending toward democracy at the level of hope." Perhaps that is why she said, "Action taken in time is the child of appropriate response: We then stop fascism as it begins, taproot by taproot in our daily lives, and never need to go to war with each other, pouring out in death our bombs, our plagues, the men and women of our future."

Is it wrong for us to hit civilian targets and kill innocent people? Of course it is. Should we view military strength and aggression as the only way to resolve conflict? Of course not. Did we do enough in the face of genocide in Africa and elsewhere? No. Do we want to send our sons and daughters into harm's way? No! But "to be against war is not enough, it is hardly a beginning," in the face of such gross human suffering perpetrated by one maniac who reminds us, all too clearly, of another. When we think of the lost children, the violated teenage girls, the blood-banked little boys, the disappeared fathers, sons, brothers, husbands, the widows who weep, the orphans who wander, the families parted from each other, the psychological trauma, the physical pain, the spiritual poverty of people who may live in a strange land but who are no strangers to the human race, how can we not act in search of "peace which is completeness"?

"We are against war," Muriel Rukeyser said. Of course we are. But when "we hear them crying to us," as the poet wrote, we must begin to "define peace, live to fight its birth, to build these meanings, to sing these songs." For without these songs, surely we have lived only at the level of hope and have failed to see that in being nonviolent, we offer our own violence to the world.

WHAT YOU REALIZE ON THE ROAD

Having returned from a splendid weekend in the Northeast Kingdom with a wonderful group of post-50 women, I realize that there are lessons to be learned everywhere. We had traveled north to see the foliage, my Crones and I, but the journey was really just another excuse to hang out together. We love each other's company, and like the notorious Ya Ya Sisterhood, we are as tight a group of "girlfriends" as you will find anywhere. We have traveled together, literally and metaphorically, over many years now, and in the midst of our sharing and laughter, our networking and support, our shopping and hiking and eating, a number of life's lessons presented themselves once again on this journey. Here are some of the more important things I learned while cruising in a camper with my pals:

1. *Friendship is truly a gift.* Some of the women I traveled with have been my friends since we were in junior high school together; one I met only recently at the Burlington airport. With each, the bonding, the

understanding, the universality of women's experience can only be classified as a treasure. There is absolutely nothing I know that is more special, more affirming, more enriching than the friendship I share with my beloved Crones, our identity tag since I turned 50 and had them all over for a pajama party that has never ended. (Some women hate the term crone, and a lot of people don't understand it. Handed down from prepatriarchal times, it refers to postmenopausal women who were revered as wise elders, and that's good enough for us.) I have long understood that often, friends are true family.

2. *There is beauty everywhere.* One of the Crones is a former Girl Scout leader, and taking a hike with her is a gateway to nature's wonders. What extraordinary perfection there is in miniature ferns that hug the forest floor. What wonders to explore in riverside rock beds. On a grander scale, I will remember forever the exquisite beauty of a mountain, fog shrouded at its top, from which snow-covered evergreen gumdrops yielded to fiery foliage on the way down to an Irish green valley lit by the sun. I have been fortunate to travel the world, and nowhere have I seen anything more moving than this Vermont scene. Beauty, I learned, is often in our very own backyards.

3. *There is joy in discovery.* If you want to remember what it was like to be a kid on a snow day, meander with your best chums through some of the small villages that dot the Vermont countryside up north. We are a pretty sophisticated group, but there was sheer happiness in the squeals of delight as the Crones explored antique shops, village stores, food emporia, and the Stowe Craft Fair. No toddler could have been more excited over a bar of scented soap, an old faux jeweled pin, or an antique "Ginny Doll." Beyond material rewards, we also reveled in nature's gifts—a

soothing waterfall, the smell of newly mown wet grass, the sight of migrating geese, being there "when the cows come home." There is always something new to discover.

4. *Communication is critical.* If you doubt this, try traveling in a 28-foot camper with five other people, even if they are your best friends. Caring, compromise, and consideration are essential. It can mean so much when someone offers you the best bunk or takes over cooking and cleaning up when you're tired or says, "Do we really want to do this?" We've had a lot of practice together in gaining consensus (women generally do). Still, a little checking goes a long way. At a deeper level, the kind of sharing the Crones do about our lives, our work, our families, ourselves, our politics is something so special that I wish it for everyone I know and love. Talking it over is really a great way to get "up close and personal."

5. *Laughter really is great medicine.* Being with the Crones (or any group of wonderful friends) is like spending a week with Patch Adams. I can't think of a healthier way to feel good, and I can honestly say that I never laugh as much as I do when I'm with this gang of women. It's not just that we tell jokes. We simply see the humor in everything, especially ourselves and each other. What a joy it is to share one's foibles, to work through some difficulty with laughter, to see the funny side of life so that its pain is more bearable.

Luckily, I get to laugh with the Crones at least twice a year, even though we live in various parts of the eastern U.S. We make a concerted effort to meet up somewhere because we simply can't make it through too long a time without being together. And no matter where we are, our communion sustains us and reminds us that very often, life's lessons are no farther away than our own back gardens or best friends.

INSIDE MOMS

They shuffle into the room, paper and pen in hand. Sitting at the table, some smile tentatively. Very few of them look directly at me. They are cautiously expectant; I am a promised diversion. While we have little in common with each other, together they share many things: drugs, abuse, past violence, or a crime committed. They are marginal, I am mainstream. I know this as I write "Welcome to the Writer's Group!" on the blackboard and begin my monthly workshop at a Vermont women's correctional facility.

I know nothing about these women individually, who come in assorted sizes, shapes, and ages, except this: They love their children with a passion unexceeded by that of anyone on the outside, and that is something we all understand; it is the great equalizer. We are bound by knowing that each one of us would die for our kids, and there is nothing in the whole world we long for more than to see our children safe and happy. It never fails. No matter what writing assignment I offer, what inspirational piece I read, what story I tell to get us started, invariably these women write about what they know best—the love they bear for their children, and the memories of their own mothers and "nanas."

American society is notoriously cruel to mothers. Having brainwashed us that our singular God-given role in life is to bear and care for our young, the "experts" then set about convincing us what a terrible job we do. It's a no-win situation. White middle-class women are told to embrace stay-at-home momism, while poor and (usually) minority women are admonished to get off their welfare duffs and go to work (the absence of transportation, child care, and skills training notwithstanding). Childhood angst is always Mom's fault, one way or another—we give them either too much love and protection or not enough. One friend of mine went through years of mother-blaming guilt only to learn that her child's behavior was the result of reactive autism; another found out that her adopted son had fetal alcohol syndrome. The latest in this diatribe is a newly released study that correlates aggressive behavior in children to placement in day care. (Even the study's authors admit that there are numerous other variables to consider and that correlation is not causation, but the media have chosen not to go into those murky details.) This study follows the "Mommy Track" and other assorted guilt trips for moms that come to us care of the only industrialized nation in the world that just can't bear to accept the idea of mothers working outside the home.

Whether we choose to stay at home or not, whether we are inside or out, motherhood can be a lonely and difficult business. Very few of us believe that we usually do a worthy job of it, and we are seldom given a pat on the back, let alone an annual review. There's no water cooler for sharing ideas and frustrations, and the bonuses are sometimes few and far between. It's a solitary occupation for which we are largely hyped, little trained, and totally unrecognized.

Nothing makes me more aware of this reality than when I listen to my prison workshop participants as they read their poems and stories of remembrance and love. Bending over their papers as if to protect them from invasion, and often with tears in their eyes, they recall the pain and pleasure of being a mother. They worry, they gloat, they hope. They transform—not only themselves, but me. I become no longer an outsider, a mentor or model; I am just a mom who understands what they are saying and feeling.

So I'd like to pay tribute to moms everywhere. And I can think of no better way to do so than by sharing the words of writer June Jordan. "Everybody's momma done better than anybody had any right to expect," she said. "And that's the truth!"

We mommas need to remember that, and so do those who try to make us think otherwise. We may not be perfect, but you can be sure of one thing: Nobody will ever love you the way we do, and that's the honest-to-God inside truth.

"TELL JAKE TO SLEEP ON THE ROOF"

Poor Margaret Sanger must be turning in her grave. Were she alive today, the founder of the internationally successful family planning movement would no doubt have wept at President Bush's first official act: rescinding foreign assistance funds to any organization providing abortions, counseling, or information on pregnancy termination overseas. Bush's father, of course, and President Reagan before him had imposed the same sanctions, lifted during the Clinton administration.

The Messrs. Bush and Reagan, it seems, have no idea about the reality of life for most women on the face of the earth. Here are a few facts it would be wise for them and other abortion opponents to contemplate: Throughout the developing world, more than 500,000 women die—that's nearly one woman every minute of every day—due to preventable causes related to childbirth. Every day, more than 31,000 children under the age of 5 die in these countries from low birth weight or other pregnancy-related complications. Birth spacing and pregnancy termination in very young and older women alone could dramatically reduce these numbers. The fact is that at least one in four maternal and infant deaths in the developing world could be prevented by family planning, safe abortions, and counseling. Further, population pressures continue to grow in many developing countries, where 95 percent of population growth occurs, contributing to deforestation, water and food shortages, and other environmental concerns. Maternal and child health care is clearly related to a world population projected to reach 8 billion by 2050 if family planning services continue to be offered, and more than 11 billion if not. But this argument is not about population control. It is about the human face of what happens to women when reproductive options are not available.

As a nurse, Margaret Sanger saw the suffering faces of these women, and it was more than she could tolerate without taking action. The watershed event for her, which ultimately led to her founding the organization that later became the International Planned Parenthood Federation, occurred when she was called to help save the life of a tenement wife named Mrs. Sachs. At 28 years of age, Mrs. Sachs already had three children. She had tried to induce abortion when pregnant with her fourth, and now she lay perilously close to death from infection. After three weeks of round-the-clock care by Sanger, Mrs. Sachs begged her doctor to tell her how she could keep from becoming pregnant again. "Tell Jake to sleep on the roof," the doctor replied. Deeply troubled, Sanger promised to return to talk to Mrs. Sachs. But before she could make good on her promise, Mrs. Sachs died from attempting to abort her fifth pregnancy. It was then, Sanger wrote in her autobiography, that she knew she had to do something.

I am of an age to remember, as Susan Brownmiller puts it, "one million women [who] braved the unknown every year, relying on a grapevine of whispers and misinformation to terminate their pregnancies by illegal means." I know what it was like before 1973 when the Supreme Court via *Roe v.*

Wade gave women in this country the constitutional right to terminate a pregnancy. I have covered for friends who fled, alone, to Puerto Rico in the hope that a hanger would not be their salvation. I have counseled married friends and referred them to safe providers once they reached that most tormented of decisions. I have heard the horror stories of hemorrhage and infertility first hand. And like all those women who bore witness and told their stories in the 1960s and 1970s, I am terrified of what might lie ahead if President Bush and his cronies have their way with women's bodies and with their wrenching private decisions, whether they are American or not.

A hundred years ago, Margaret Sanger wrote simply: "A woman has the right to control her own body." How astounding, and frightening, that a century later we must still fight for that right, no matter where we live, and absolutely irrespective of where Jake chooses to sleep.

BUDDHAS AND BURKAHS

Like the rest of the world, I was appalled by the willful destruction of ancient Buddhas by repressive Taliban thugs in Afghanistan. I applaud the quick and collective cry of outrage that has reverberated around the globe against a cruel and unenlightened regime that saw fit to destroy extraordinary art treasures that were a legacy for all humankind. Would that such cries of outrage had been heard over the willful destruction of women's lives in that tragic country.

The Universal Declaration of Human Rights promulgated by the United Nations in the 1940s states that "everyone has the right to a standard of living adequate for the health and well-being of self and family, including food, clothing, housing and medical care and necessary social services, and the right to security in the event of . . . sickness, disability, widowhood, old age or other circumstances." Nevertheless, in Afghanistan, as in no other crisis spot in the world, women have been subjected to an unprecedented loss of human and civil rights, and for the most part, the world has remained silent.

This wall of silence obscures the reality of gender apartheid in Afghanistan, but in Pakistani camps, refugees tell horrific stories. They include reports of ethnic cleansing, trafficking in women and girls, sexual slavery of both girls and boys, slaughter, and mayhem. Ever since the Taliban militia took over their country in 1996, Afghan women, more than any other group, have been brutally and systematically suppressed. They may not work, attend school, leave home without a close male relative, or seek medical attention. The windows of their homes are painted black. They are required to wear the suffocating *burkah*, a dark, heavy robe that obscures them completely and through which they can barely see. If so much as a hand or an ankle accidentally shows or if sandals or the wrong color socks are worn, women are beaten, or worse. One woman who was gang-raped tried to commit suicide by jumping from a building. When she did not die, she drank a caustic substance to complete the deed. Depression is pervasive, suicide is rampant, and old women go begging. Says one aid worker, "there is brutal enforcement of gender apartheid restrictions. But none of the world's governments have made an issue of it." She worries that if terrorist Osama bin Laden, who is headquartered in Afghanistan, were to be turned over to the West, sanctions against the country would be lifted and what little attention has been paid to the plight of women would soon disappear.

Ossai Miazad is a native of Afghanistan who immigrated to the U.S. in 1976 when the Russians invaded her country. She remembers when things were different. "We were making advances," she recalls. "Women were allowed to get an education, government agencies were open to them, it was a country in progress. Now, when I hear the news, I realize how little separates me from those women. Literally, one evening in my life made the difference between me and another woman trapped there now."

The situation is devastating for children as well as women. According to UNICEF, a majority of Afghan children suffer from severe stress as a result of witnessing violence, including the killing of their parents. In the most heavily land-mined country in the world, 10 to 12 people lose their lives or are maimed daily, many of them children. It falls to the women to care for these disabled children while they themselves are traumatized, malnourished, and secluded.

The 1994 UN *Human Development Report* defines human development as a process of widening the range of people's choices. Human development, it says, should "empower people, enabling them to design and participate in the process and events that shape their lives."

For Afghan women, these are bitter words. They know that their rights have been subordinated to a political agenda of which they are no part. Thoroughly disillusioned and debilitated, and with nothing left to lose, they mourn not the destruction of art but the destruction of their own lives and the demise of hope.

Surely the very least we can do is to join them in their grief and to remind our own governments that, in the end, life is art.

TRAFFIC JAM

The death of 16-year-old Christal Jones, a Vermont teenager slain in a seedy brothel in New York City, is sadly just the tip of a growing iceberg. On a national or global scale, the trafficking in women for sexual slavery—for that is what it is—reveals an alarming trend.

According to the United Nations, trafficking is now more lucrative than the international trade in illicit weapons. The UN estimated that procurers, smugglers, and corrupt officials who supplied the emerging international trade in human beings made $7 billion in profits from their human cargo in 1997. Approximately 4 million women, children, and men become victims of international trafficking each year. Some young girls are sold into prostitution by their destitute families; others are duped into slavery by fraudulent "employment brokers" who promise legitimate work to those eager to escape economic hardship. Whether under the guise of domestic servant or sweatshop laborer, as many as 100,000 female victims are forced into prostitution each year, according to the U.S. Department of State. Other sources believe that the number of victims coerced into the sex trade worldwide is much higher.

Trafficking usually flows from poorer to wealthier regions; from rural to urban settings. It used to be a fairly local affair; now it is global big business. Eastern European women are sent to Western Europe, the U.S., the Near East, the Far East. In South and Southeast Asia, where sexual slavery is rampant and involves ever younger prey, international crime syndicates now have a piece of the action. Brokers find victims (who have often been kidnaped), others secure travel documents, smugglers transport people, corrupt officials cooperate, children disappear. In virtually all cases, force and coercion are central to the effort. "Victims are compelled into activities they cannot refuse and under conditions they cannot control. Fear and force drive what happens," says the Office of Women in Development at the U.S. Agency for International Development. Here's how it usually works: A recruiter shows up in a rural village advertising jobs for anything from domestic servants to "entertainment workers." A young girl, pretty and shy, expresses interest. The recruiter offers her parents a cash advance against future earnings. She is whipped away with promises of all the money she will be sending home to help her struggling family. Soon, the young victim finds herself in debt to her "employer," a debt she can never clear. Afraid, she does not seek legal counsel or other help. Within a year, she has probably had at least one coerced abortion, and she is likely to be HIV-positive. According to the Brussels-based International Organization for Migration, as many as half a million women and girls were trafficked into Western Europe for forced prostitution in this way in 1996.

In Germany, to take one example, tabloid advertisements offer "sexy Czech [who] makes housecalls" and "Russian beauty [who] gives erotic massage." If caught, the "sexy Czech" and the "Russian beauty" are taken into custody and deported, if they're lucky; their abusers go free. Germany offers no witness protection program. For the most part, its churches "don't want to admit the problem exists," says a representative of a women's center that runs a hotline for victims, and political authorities and the media are conspicuously silent.

According to one European women's advocate, captive women are often raped and beaten into submission. "All the while they are photographed. The recruiters threaten to send the photos home to their families if they go to the police or try to escape." One German authority reported that torture and other scare tactics, like hanging women out of windows, were used.

Twenty-one-year-old Nadia, from Ukraine, is a real woman caught in this scenario. In a documented interview, she told a reporter she has "moral problems." She wants to go home.

Christal Jones probably wanted to go home too. But for her, like so many others, it is too late.

People don't think such things happen here. As Vermont's Governor Howard Dean said, "This is not the thing that one normally associates with Vermont." But the prostitution ring Christal was victim to is a strong signal that organized trafficking of women and girls is real, and it is on the rise everywhere. It behooves us all to know that, and to register our contempt and alarm.

A JURY OF HER PEERS, ALMOST

There are 213 of us, and we all wish we were somewhere else. So the clerk in the yellow suit advises us not to try rescheduling. The last guy who did that, she says, ended up serving on a three-month instead of a three-day trial. At this, a few businessmen roll their eyes upward and slump down in their seats as if to escape being seen. Some young mothers clutch their throats in alarm. Most go on reading their newspapers and romance novels, unscathed by the idea that they may be held captive indefinitely. The clerk, perky as a sparrow in a mine shaft, gives us the drill and then rolls a videotape that repeats everything she just said.

She disappears. A while later, she reemerges, commanding "numbers 70 through 110, report to courtroom 15, sixth floor!" Figures. I have just returned from the caverns of the courthouse basement with a cup of coffee that must now be abandoned. This is my third call for jury duty. The first time I was summoned, my feminist credentials ensured my dismissal; the second time, a mistrial ended my day in court before it began. This time, I'm ambivalent about the call to serve. I believe the jury system is an important piece of democratic society. I also think the notion of a "jury of your peers" is a joke; it is anything but, once the lawyers finish. But I am intrigued by the system. I want to experience the process from the perspective of a juror, having already acted the role of witness, ironically, as it will turn out, in a sex discrimination case.

The judge enters the chamber, a smallish place as courtrooms go, bowed at the front and woodpaneled. All rise, then sit again. We are read the charges in the case—two counts of harassment—and the names of the plaintiff, the defendant, and the witnesses. Then the selection begins. As the black-robed judge, an amiable sort of chap who looks only slightly bored by his daily routine, asks a series of questions—"Have any of you ever been the victim of a violent crime? Have any of you ever served on a jury before? Is there anyone here whose opinion of the jury system would preclude them serving as a juror? Is there anyone present who has knowledge of any of the people connected to this case?"—various members of our group rise, one by one, and request permission to approach the bench. Under protection of a scramble device that fills the room with maddeningly secretive static, they whisper to the judge and the lawyers, guaranteeing that their services will not be required. I wonder if I should confess my doubts about jury selection and decide against it. Finally 12 of us are seated, 4 of whom are replaced before the swearing in, an attempt by the plaintiff's attorney, it seems, to seat more women than men.

The defendant, a nerd of a guy in a blue suit and sneakers, sits passively through the entire procedure, peering expressionlessly through his plastic-framed glasses at the table where he and his lawyer sit. His eyes appear lifeless, without threat, yet there is something unsettling, a hint of contempt perhaps. His thinning hair above a pale, pasty face makes him look like an oversized schoolboy, the kind of kid who probably hugs the building in sullen solitude during recess and who is teased mercilessly in the locker room by the macho guys. His lawyer is also pasty-faced and gaunt, with thinning hair and an unreadable demeanor. They belong together, like salt and pepper shakers.

At the plaintiff's table, a young woman in a dark green tailored suit, white blouse, and pearls consults her documents and then looks up and smiles, apparently pleased with those of us who have been sworn in. She will prove herself a novice attorney over the course of the next few hours, but she is earnest and likable as she spars with her arrogant counterpart.

Now the judge reads us the charges again and explains our responsibility: to determine the defendant's guilt or innocence on two charges of harassment. The first charge rests in whether he had the "intent" to harass the plaintiff on a specific day, the second on whether he willfully undertook a subsequent "course of conduct" over a specific period of time despite "reasonable warning." The notions of "intent" and "reasonable warning" will lead us to more than three hours of deliberation and a nearly hung jury, but we do not know that yet.

The arguments are brief and the witnesses few. The lawyer in the green suit recounts three occasions on which the plaintiff was followed by the defendant, terrorized, we are told, as she tried to flee him in the aisles of a shop, in a mall, in a supermarket. Two policemen testify that she was weeping, shaking, traumatized, when they responded to her 911 calls. The plaintiff, a pretty woman with long hair and big eyes who appears only for her testimony, twists her wedding band around her finger and repeats the sequence of events. Then, probed, lowering her eyes, she tells us that she is afraid now to shop alone, she has nightmares, men frighten her.

The defense asks each witness a lengthy set of questions aimed, it appears, at suggesting that the encounters were random events, coincidences.

Where spectators sit, a lone old woman, a mother,

watches. Beneath her perfectly coiffed gray hair is the face of the defendant.

In closing arguments, the pasty-faced lawyer approaches the jury box, legal tome in hand. He admonishes us to pay close attention to the letter of the law, then reads us a series of definitions and says, "So, you have no case here. By definition, you cannot find the defendant guilty as charged!" He's good. Reasonable doubt creeps in, even though we all know that the man he is defending was at the mall, the supermarket, the shop, following the pretty young woman with the long hair. He is followed by the lawyer in the green suit. She says, "We all know what he was doing there! He knew what he was doing." Then she walks us through the three episodes again, but she never asks, "How did he know where she would be?" Never suggests that he must have known where she worked, what car she drove. Are we allowed to talk about this, we wonder?

At 4:00 P.M. we file into the deliberation room. Among us are a grandmother knitting a baby sweater, a speech pathologist, a brassy woman in black whose style gives feminists the label "strident," a college professor, an activist with a law degree, and a businessman. Besides him, there are four other men: one who is so eager to go home that he has no convictions, another who seems unable to think for himself, one clean-cut WASP of a guy who moves decidedly right of center as our discussion proceeds, and the foreman, patient and calm. The other two women are nondescript and silent.

The foreman reads the charges and the definitions of "intent" and "reasonable warning." We take a first vote on the second count because it seems less problematic. Eight to four: guilty. The four are men.

"Why didn't she say anything to him?" the clean-cut guy asks, wide-eyed. "Tell him to back off? That would have been reasonable warning, seems to me." We women look at each other and try not to roll our eyes. The speech pathologist explains softly that everything women are taught about such encounters advises against engagement. No eye contact. No conversation. Just get away. Find help. Get to a crowd.

"Maybe she was being provocative, what about that?" another guy says. "We don't know. Maybe she was flirting, wearing something, you know."

"I don't care if she was naked!" I say, teeth clenched. "You don't harass women."

The businessman offers a string of Talmudic arguments in which he lays out all the ramifications of what could be meant by "reasonable" and "warning."

"He's guilty!" the woman in black shouts. "I'm telling you, he harassed her, she warned him, and he just kept doing it! What's the big deal here?"

It goes on like this for over an hour. Then one by one, largely swayed by the speech pathologist, the college professor, and the lawyer-activist—none of whom are strangers to feminist thought or women's advocacy—the four men are moved to vote in favor of conviction.

On the first count, it's not so easy. The "intent" thing bogs us down, makes us send out to the judge for clarification, causes tempers to flare as we watch the hands on the clock stretch between 12 and 6. Did he know what he was doing? Did he mean to do it? Did she only think he intended to "alarm, annoy, or harass"?

"Maybe she was overreacting," someone says.

It's late, I'm tired, and I start to lose it. "Do you understand the fear women are walking around with? Do you realize how many women are dead because no one took their stalkers seriously?" I speak of the Clothesline Project, the row upon row of decorated and inscribed T-shirts commemorating women dead as a result of violence, as the AIDS Quilt remembers those lost to that carnage.

"C'mon! It's no different than if a man followed a man, or a woman followed a woman," someone pipes up. "I don't think sex has anything to do with it."

"It is a gender thing!" I rumble. I am pacing, clenching my fists to keep my voice from exploding lest I lose my credibility. "Women do not rape men!"

The woman in black and the speech pathologist chime in, one calmly, the other with shouts and a finger jabbing the air.

The businessman returns us to the meaning of "intent." At this point, he is the lone holdout. On the last count, we were at 11 to 1.

"With all respect, and as a Jew myself," I say, "we could pursue Talmudic arguments all night long, but we have a mandate, and a parameter in which to carry out that mandate."

"What's Talmudic argument?" the guy who increasingly seems like white bread asks.

"It's what the Jesuits do," says the speech pathologist, smiling at him. He looks bewildered but does not pursue it.

We go through several more rounds of dialogue and debate, growing ever more redundant. Finally, on the fine point of whether the definition of intent says "and" or "or," the Talmudic scholar yields, joining in the majority opinion. Guilty. On both counts. We send word to the judge that a verdict has been reached.

Filing back into the jury box, my eyes meet those of the defendant's mother. I am sad for her. It is a terrible thing that she is enduring. But I am absolutely sure we have deliberated well.

"Have you reached a verdict?" we are asked.

"We have," the foreman says. Each charge is read, and to each he says, "Guilty as charged." We are asked, one by one, if we concur, and we say, "I do." There is a brief discussion about when sentencing will take place, the judge expressing concern that the defendant might disappear before the date set. Finally, everyone but the judge and jury leave the room.

It is then that we learn the defendant has already been jailed for stalking and is up against further charges.

The judge thanks us. We return to the jury room to collect our belongings. The men who thought the woman with the pretty eyes and long hair might have been overreacting, or just imagining it, look sheepish. One of them apologizes and asks me to tell him again about the T-shirts on the Clothesline. We congratulate ourselves for taking our job so seriously, and we applaud the Talmudic scholar for his commitment. The system, we agree, works.

Then the speech pathologist, the college professor, the activist, and the woman in black look at each other, smile, leave the courtroom and disperse back into their own lives.

I think about the mother with the gray hair and wonder where she will spend this chilly November night.

REMEMBER THE WOMEN

In the spirit of Abigail Adams, we need to "remember the ladies," especially on International Women's Day, when we consider the state of many of the world's women. In Afghanistan, as we now know, things couldn't have been much worse if you happened to have been born female and lived under the Taliban regime. Women were prohibited from working, attending school, and, in many cases, seeking medical attention. Like thousands of women in Asia and Eastern Europe, they were often abducted, raped, and sold to sexual slavery markets, never to be seen again. Enforcement of gender apartheid was brutal. If so much as a hand or an ankle showed from beneath a *burkah,* or if sandals or the wrong color socks were worn, women were beaten, sometimes to death. In many African countries and elsewhere, young girls are subjected to brutal mutilation of their genitals for the sake of their future husbands' sexual pleasure. Two-thirds of the world's illiterate people are women. Women perform two-thirds of the world's work, yet they earn one-tenth of the world's income and own less than one-one hundredth of the world's property. If you wonder what this has to do with women in the U.S. and other industrialized nations, think again: Although women constitute 52 percent of the world's population, they hold less than 13 percent of the seats in the 179 parliaments of the world and only about 10 percent are Fortune 500 corporate officers are women. The U.S. has yet to pass an Equal Rights Amendment or to ratify the international Convention to Eliminate All Forms of Discrimination Against Women. There's more where those data come from, but you get the picture.

I was reminded of the contributions women make in all societies when I read about the "personnel crisis" in the Catholic Church, which is having a devil of a time (pun intended) recruiting young nuns. It seems that the number of nuns in the U.S. has "fallen like a stone," and with the median age of American nuns being 68, that's a worry. The Church has finally had to concede that "sisters really did build the American Catholic Church through their teaching in the parochial school system and their staffing of Catholic hospitals. They have been the backbone of the church in this century . . . who will succeed them?" *(New York Times,* January 15, 2000*).* And that's not to mention all the nuns who spent their careers peeling potatoes so that priests might eat.

Similarly, the vast majority of health care workers in the world are women. Just think about it: Where would hospitals and other facilities be without the women who prepare the meals, do the laundry, provide the nursing care, staff the labs, clean the halls, offer physical and occupational therapy, and so on? And by the way, it was women's activism that led to the establishment of the Food and Drug Administration and to getting a grip on the out-of-control number of hysterectomies, C-sections, radical mastectomies, and overdosing of women with psychotropic drugs that ran rampant not so long ago.

You could say the same about women's role in education (where over 90 percent of teachers are women, but most principals and superintendents are men) or any number of other sectors of society. Because in our triple roles as producers, reproducers, and community workers, the fact is that without women's labor, the world would simply stop ticking day after day after day.

So this year, on International Women's Day (March 8), or any other day of the year for that matter, stop a moment to remember the women in your life. Thank them for all they've done for you, for your family, and for the community where you live. Abigail Adams, and all the rest of us, would be very grateful.

WAITING FOR THE FAT LADY TO SING

As baseball great Yogi Berra used to say, "It ain't over till it's over." And as far as I can see, where women are concerned, it ain't over by a long shot.

Anyone who thinks that institutionalized misogyny is a thing of the past should think again. Or ask the more than 40 women who were accosted in New York's Central Park in broad daylight while the cops stood around twiddling their nightsticks. Or perhaps consider what Southern Baptists had to say about women serving as pastors. Can it really be that in the 21st century women are still expected to "submit graciously" to their husbands?

The Reverend Adrian Rogers, chairman of the committee that drafted his church's recent statement of faith, isn't alone in his belief that "leadership is male." Just take a look at the makeup of the U.S. Congress, the number of women who head Fortune 500 companies, the top positions at the United Nations, the percentage of female school principals and superintendents, and so on. Nor are the New York City police a rare breed who thought that the gals might have been overreacting to some Sunday-in-the-park fun. Not by a long shot.

In fact, the history of patriarchy (sorry, fellas, but that is the word for it) is well documented by such credible historians as Gerda Lerner and Riane Eisler, who have spent their professional lives researching and documenting the fact that women have always been perceived as downright dangerous and inferior. (Let's face it: The only way to overcome fear of the enemy is to make the enemy inferior.) In her excellent book *At the Root of This Longing*, Carol Lee Flinders explores the relationship between feminism and spirituality and, in so doing, adds to our understanding of a phenomenon that has kept women at society's margins: "For one group of people to be fully 'authorized,' others have to be subordinate to them—'commodified' and 'reified' in one way or another: controlled, or simply silenced . . . . Women's subordination doesn't have to be policed, for it has achieved the perfect balance between force and finesse."

The force of the men who assaulted 44 women and the finesse of the Baptist brothers who assured their womenfolk that there would always be a role for them in the church speak volumes in support of Flinders's claim that "the dissociation and the disconnection from others afflicting women today are system wide." System wide, very sad, and ultimately frightening. For in thousands of years of human history, everything—and nothing—has changed. "The path of renunciation is women's daily lot," as French philosopher Luce Irigaray once observed.

And in that renunciation lies our fear of an afternoon in the park, our foreclosure at the alter, our quietly forceful exclusion from many of the establishments of our time. Not until this reality is part of our history, a thing of the past about which we are all ashamed and amazed, will women really be free to be who they are, to go where they wish, to relinquish silence.

Perhaps when they do let go of that silence, it will not

only be the fat lady who sings; it will be a chorus of women joyfully raising their voices.

A sweeter sound I cannot imagine.

BOYS WILL BE BOYS, BUT FOR HOW LONG?

First there was Aristotle, who declared, "We should regard female nature as afflicted with a natural defectiveness." St. Thomas thought of women as "incidental beings." Martin Luther believed that "with tricks and cunning, women deceive men," and 18th-century Lord Chesterfield declared that women "are only children of a larger growth." Nietzsche proposed that "woman was God's second mistake," and Freud declared females "ethically abnormal." In short, there is nothing new about misogyny.

What is new is the form it is taking, especially among our youth. In the good old days, woman-hating was occasionally demonstrated in heinous ways. For example, husbands could commit their wives to insane asylums simply for disagreeing with them. But for the most part, it is safe to say that overt acts of violence against women were the exception. Misogyny generally reared its ugly, unenlightened head in the form of myth and mind-numbing expectation. Women were viewed as fickle, fragile, and morally inferior; the good wife was expected to remain dependent, depressed, and delusional in the privacy of her boudoir. But neither the plaything nor the "angel in the house" was singled out for sexual attack.

Today, date rape is big on college campuses. A debacle at Dartmouth is a case in point. Zeta Psi fraternity newsletters—"an institution" as one frat brother called them—were confiscated for printing articles like "More Gratuitous Cancun Porn" and "Sigma Report." These pieces described fraternity members' sexual escapades with women, sported photographs of bare-breasted coeds, and, perhaps most disturbingly, promised "patented date rape techniques" in a future issue. (Ironically, the newsletters were leaked during Sexual Awareness Week at the Ivy League inspiration for the 1978 film *Animal House.*) When asked to comment on the articles, fraternity members are reported to have shrugged them off, claiming, "Boys will be boys." One former Zeta Psi member reported that such newsletters were distributed regularly and were part of a "tradition held in the greatest esteem." The fraternity's president denied that the newsletters had threatened or harassed women in any way and whined that closing the fraternity, as Dartmouth authorities did, was "overly harsh and grossly disproportionate to the offenses charged." In perhaps the greatest insult of all, he claimed that the newsletters were internal documents and constituted "humor, satire, and parody." Some sense of humor.

But the problem doesn't stop at the frat house door. It goes to the sorority houses and the dorms, to the bars where college kids hang out, to the parties they attend, to the entire social fabric of our time. The question is not only Why are boys and men behaving like this in the 21st century? It is also Why are girls and young women buying into a culture that so degrades them?

Certainly there are feisty feminists out there who don't participate in the feeding frenzy of sex, pornography, and sickening dominatrix ads in glossy girlie magazines. But an awful lot of nice kids can't seem not to buy into such dissipation, even if solely as observers. I have been alarmed and saddened by reading the journals my Women's Studies students write. They share stories of spring-break orgies, bars that pay girls to take off their shirts, nude picture-taking, binge-drinking sex. They are stunned, perhaps even sickened, by what they see, but few of them are willing to act on their own behalf. The majority remain complicit in their passivity. "Boys will be boys," they say, in one way or another.

And that is why I am alarmed, and sad. For if this group of self-selected and often savvy college women can't speak out against such degradation, if they too bemoan their looks, agonize over their love lives, and let their boyfriends dictate what they will wear and how they will act, then who will bear the banner of "Enough is enough!" Who will teach the younger sisters that it isn't necessary (or appropriate) to do Britney Spears in an undershirt to garner attention? Who will stand up to the Zeta Psi fraternities of the world and proclaim that date rape is not funny and woman-hating is no private laughing matter?

After the fraternity was closed down, some of the Dartmouth boys claimed that their free speech rights had been impinged upon. (Poor babies.) Perhaps if a few more girls would exercise their own free speech, guys in and out of frat houses would come to understand not only that the days of "you're cute when you're angry" are over, but also that violence against and sexual harassment of women are no more appropriate now than the flicker of a gas lamp in an age of electric connection.

A MOVEMENT CONTINUES

As writer Ellen Goodman observed, "people have been writing premature obituaries on the women's movement since its beginning." This seems a good time to remind readers that women, and men, who adhere to the radical notion that women's rights are human rights are very much alive, and kicking more ferociously than ever.

A lot of us are old enough to remember what it was like in the bad old days of the 1940s and 1950s, when, as Susan Brownmiller points out, "Help Wanted columns were divided into Male for the jobs with a future, and Female for the dead-end positions; . . . pretty young unmarried women with a taste for adventure were recruited to trundle a meal cart down the aisle of an airplane but weren't allowed to train as pilots; . . . a male-only admissions policy excluded the brightest and most talented female students; and . . . a teaching certificate or nursing degree was 'something to fall back on.'"

But we also remember the early days of our feminist organizing, and that Aha! moment when we realized, as Carol Hanisch put it in 1968, that "the personal is political." Ruth Rosen, in her book *The World Split Open*, explains: "By this she meant to convey the then-shocking idea that there were political dimensions to private life, that power relations shaped life in marriage, in the kitchen, the bedroom, the nursery, and at work." Rosen recalls the excitement we all felt in telling our own stories: "By questioning 'the natural order of things,' women began to see their conditions through their own eyes. Why, for example, did men enjoy more leisure time? Why were women's fingers considered perfectly suited for making small widgets on an assembly line, but not for neurosurgery? Why did women clean the toilet while men cut the grass?" Through consciousness-raising sessions, "suddenly, one 'got it.' This isn't just my problem!"

Imagine, then, what it must have been like back in 1848 when women like Susan B. Anthony, Elizabeth Cady Stanton, and Matilda Joslyn Gage envisioned an egalitarian society in which married women might own property, in which they need not fear that their children could be taken from them through the arbitrary wishes of their husbands, in which they might vote. What courage it took to stand before a body of men and ask, as Stanton did, "Who, I ask you, can take, dare take, on himself the rights, the duties, the responsibilities of another human soul?" Or for a former slave to declare, as Sojourner Truth did, "I wish woman to have her voice!"

For that matter, think of the 1920 drama of waiting to hear from a lone young man in the Tennessee state legislature, on whose vote women's suffrage rested. "Don't forget to be a good boy . . . vote for suffrage," his mother had written to 24-year-old Harry Burn. When the roll call in the tied House reached him, he voted to ratify, ending 72 years of struggle to enfranchise half the adult population of America.

No less dramatic were the words, writings, and actions of social activists and analysts like Charlotte Perkins Gilman, Margaret Sanger, and Eleanor Roosevelt, to name but a few.

These women worked hard so that, in ER's words, "the people of this country could be reached with the truth."

The torch lit by 19th century suffragists and passed so gallantly to 20th century feminists, many of whom suffered extraordinary indignities simply to obtain the right to vote, burned brightly into the 1960s and 1970s, and it burns brightly still. Bella Abzug, Betty Friedan, Gloria Steinem are but a few of the names we associate with progress in recognizing the full dignity and place of women in all societies. Rebecca Walker now follows in the footsteps of her mother, Alice, as my daughter Rachel follows in mine. They go on, because there is still work to be done. As Charlotte Perkins Gilman once said of the young, "They shall be like a vast reserve force to a tired army. They will lift the world forward. They will bring fresh new powers to bear."

I look around me, and I know that the women's movement is not dead. Rather, it is in the capable hands of the so-called Third Wave. I respect them, I trust them with the legacy, and I wish them Godspeed.

MOTHERS AND MANAGERS: WORKING IT OUT

I wouldn't want to be in Jane Swift's shoes, and not because she just had twins. The acting governor of Massachusetts has a difficult situation to deal with, and her dilemma is important to all women who want both work and family in their lives. The question for Ms. Swift is, How will she reconcile having three children under the age of 4 as well as a critically important career that clearly means a great deal to her? And how will she deal with the flack she is getting for trying?

Not so very long ago, Freud asked that all-important question: What do women want? The answer is really quite simple—we want it all, just like men. We want the twin engines of life, which is to say, love and work. We want to nurture our intellects without having to say bye-bye to our parenting instincts. We want a full and complete life, with all its inherent challenges and opportunities.

The backlash against women who struggle with this dual goal has been harsh, and Swift is the latest victim in the annals of male resistance to working moms, a concept that we

Americans see as the ultimate oxymoron (not realizing that no one works harder than stay-at-home moms). Conservatives are only too eager to use Ms. Swift's situation as a way to prove that women with small children can't have it all, no matter what they think. Her husband Charles Hunt, of course, comes under no such scrutiny. When was the last time someone asked him how he was going to cope with colic or three-hour commutes? Who would suggest that his conference calls were not legitimate?

For the record, former governor and Boston mayor James M. Curley conducted mayoral business for five months in 1947 from a jail cell (where he was incarcerated for mail fraud), and no one thought he was ineffective. Nor are audio or video conferences unconstitutional, as some have suggested.

At the same time, young women with high-profile professional careers must consider the reality that the Swift situation represents, and I'm the first to admit it. Some years ago my feminist ideology was put to the test when a friend and colleague of mine had a baby six weeks prematurely. A problematic pregnancy meant that my friend had had to cut back to part time, which was not in the original plan. Then her maternity leave commenced before we had anticipated it and lasted longer than expected, throwing the rest of us off balance. We compensated nicely, everyone cheerfully chipping in to fill the gap her sudden departure had created. But when a major set of documents had to be produced, tensions ran high in the office, and I could understand why. As a manager, I sympathized with the people I was supervising, who were well on the road to burnout. At the same time, I wanted to support the new mother, who had her hands full at home while worrying about how we were coping on her behalf. When I grew weary of doing her work as well as my own, I couldn't let on. It seemed disloyal on all counts.

I felt guilty whenever I was angry about the dilemma. I

wanted to be a good feminist and a good manager. But as hard as I grappled with those two roles, reconciling them wasn't easy. It still isn't. It would help, of course, if we had in place support systems that foster dual-career family life, the kind of thing that Sweden does so well. Just relinquishing our Victorian mores would go a long way toward resolving much of the problem, were we able to translate such progressive thinking into public policy. So far, we have not been willing to try that.

So I wish Jane Swift, who has a lot more support than most mothers do, all the best with her budding family and her bright future. I would like all those reactionary conservative thinkers to get off her case and focus on what's really important. I have every confidence that the great state of Massachusetts will weather their governor's giving birth just fine.

What I am less sure about is this: How do you manage to have it all when the patriarchy persists in perpetuating mythological motherhood?

And another thing: When deadlines loom, who's going to do what by when?

It's never been simple. Somehow, mothers and managers will just have to work it out.

MARTYR MOMS, MANLY MOTIVES: WOMEN AND THE GLOBAL ECONOMY

With the annual meetings of the World Bank and the International Monetary Fund (IMF) shortened from a week to a weekend because of demonstration worries, it seems timely to remember how women fit into the dialogue around globalization, world economics, and transnational business interests.

New Zealand economist and former member of parliament Marilyn Waring first opened feminist eyes to women's invisibility in this sphere with her 1988 book *If Women Counted.* Her opening vignette is worth sharing. It is about a young girl in Zimbabwe who starts her day at 4 A.M. when, in order to get water, she carries a 30-liter tin to a borehole about 11 kilometers from her home. She returns at 9 A.M., eats a little, and proceeds to collect firewood until midday. Then she cleans, prepares lunch, cleans up again, fetches wild vegetables for supper, makes a second trip for water, prepares supper, puts the younger children to bed, and toes to sleep herself at 9 P.M. Yet her work is not counted in Zimbabwe's national system of accounting. She is considered "unproductive, unoccupied, and economically inactive" because no cash value has been placed on her work.

In the North American version of this story, a young, middle-class "housewife" shops for food, prepares and serves several meals a day, cleans house, cares for children, does laundry, chauffeurs, pays bills, looks after plants and animals, makes repairs, fields phone calls, possibly gardens, and often takes care of elderly parents. She too is considered unproductive, unoccupied, and economically inactive.

Nancy Folbre, author of *The Invisible Heart: Economics and Family Values* (New Press, 2001), understands this scenario, and like many of us, she is outraged. "Caregivers in general and mothers in particular subsidize the market economy. And that market economy is sucking them dry, just as it is sucking up other natural resources like clean air, sea turtles, tropical hardwoods, and a stable climate. It's time for the market economy to get weaned, grasp the meaning of 'no,' learn to use the potty and offer some pay-back."

In her book, Folbre points out that the relative costs of caring for others are going up, posing problems for sustaining the long-term economy. "Instead of chattering on about the 'new economy' or 'value investing,'" she argues, "we should focus attention on the 'care sector'" of our economy. This sector bridges unpaid and paid work. It includes the labor provided within families and communities in the 'informal' economy and the largely underpaid work of childcare, elder care, nursing, teaching, and social services in the formal economy."

Folbre underscores that women have been subject to the "care penalty" because they see intrinsic value in caring for others, because they lack the skills to do other work, and because the work just needs to be done. Economists and businesspeople like to coo about women's "psychic income," she says, but ask any minimum-wage mom how that puts food on the table.

We need to remember that care, like other resources, is not infinite. It gets used up, depleted, tired. That's why the turnover rates in schools, nursing homes, day-care centers, and hospitals are so high. It's why the church can't recruit nuns, nursing school enrollment is down, teachers are hard to find. And yet, now comes the return of patriarchy under Mr. Bush and his cronies, who really believe that a woman's place is in the home (unless she is out volunteering for a faith-based charity of her choice). Why aren't more people up in arms? Because, says Folbre, patriarchy saves money. It's good for business. Analyst Felicia Kronbluh puts it this way: "Assigning waged work primarily to one group and caring to another saves money because the care workers are systematically unpaid or underpaid. The care workers, disproportionately female, absorb a vast portion of the necessary costs of a capitalist economy. Employers, governments, and individual men all benefit." According to Kronbluh, the National Family Caregivers Association estimates that if individuals or companies paid for them, the services of family caregivers in the U.S. alone would cost $196 billion a year. Further, the value of nonmarket work is estimated to be between 30 and 60 percent of all goods and services in the U.S.

What happens to all that saved money, anyway? Ever wonder how the defense budget got so big? How companies manage to move entire manufacturing plants to low-wage countries? How some guys can afford that midlife Mercedes?

Young feminists are beginning to see this light. They nix volunteering that isn't activist and ask for an end to "martyr moms." "We need to stop selling ourselves for free," as the 20-something authors of the book *Manifesta* put it. Often, they say, women volunteer to do the jobs that government ought to be funding, such as tutoring, offering victim services, or being docents at museums. "Selflessness and good works are important," say authors Jennifer Baumgardner and Amy

Richards, "but in the context of women's rights, unpaid and selfless volunteer labor can be a misuse of women's energy, perpetuating the myth that women's issues are somehow less important."

It isn't easy for women to say "Enough!" As Folbre puts it, "The prisoner of care also stares out from behind the bars of social policy." And can you imagine a welfare mother "insisting that fathers take custody of the children, [or] putting them up for adoption, [or] dropping them off at an orphanage?" Folbre asks.

This is the stuff of real life, and I'm not optimistic that it will be discussed at the World Bank and IMF meetings. I suspect that not one of the (mostly) men gathered there will have read Folbre's book, or Waring's, or Ann Crittenden's *The Price of Motherhood.* How many of them have listened, really listened, to ordinary Third World women's testimonies of work, caregiving, or community responsibilities? How many will dare to think about the possibility of World Trade Organization—mandated shorter workweeks, paid leaves for family caretakers, or other models for valuing women's contributions to the global economy?

The reality is that the current excitement about global markets, capital, and labor far exceeds any concerns about family welfare. Globalization and international economics will be driven, as always, by the profit motive, leaving Folbre and others like her pessimistic. "The new global order," she says, "seems to offer two equally unattractive choices: we can go back to a patriarchal society where women are forced to assume the burden of care, or we can move ahead to a world where individuals are on their own and nobody provides care unless it is paid for in carefully calibrated low-cost units. Reasonable alternatives are hard to imagine, and harder to implement. But they are worth fighting for."

Absolutely. But something tells me that it will be women who take up that fight too, in between their myriad other responsibilities caring for home, hearth, husband, and community.

OUTING MEDEA

I was one of the lucky ones. My postpartum depression was agonizingly prolonged, but I was among the 30 percent of new mothers whose depression, while clinically severe, is self-limited. Unlike the 10 percent of women who slide into psychosis, we don't go truly crazy. We just feel like life is over.

In Greek mythology, Medea is well known, and despised, because she kills her two sons to revenge her husband. But in one version of the tragedy, she murders them to save them from death at the hands of others; she is choosing what she believes to be the lesser of two terrible evils for her children.

Perhaps that was the perception of Andrea Yates when she drowned her five children in Houston. Maybe in her despair she thought that if she could no longer care for them they would be taken away from her, so she took them away herself. Who can say? Our minds play awful tricks on us when they are deeply disturbed.

What was in the mind of Aracely Erives, who gave birth to quadruplets in Chicago and then drowned herself in Lake Michigan a week later? What was Melanie Stokes, also of Chicago, thinking when she jumped to her death from a twelfth-story hotel window after her baby was born? How could Lisa Anderson, saved from suicide through therapy and antidepressants, have thought, after the birth of her third child, that her family would be better off without her?

We know precious little about postpartum depression, but one thing is certain: It is a precarious psychological state that we must begin to better understand. We need to take seriously the pain and confusion some women experience in the period of exhaustion after childbirth. We must offer them respite so that they, and their children, can survive.

Some years ago, women's advocates brought domestic violence out of the closet. Then we began to acknowledge the sexual abuse of children, enabling them to seek and find help. Elder abuse, in families and in institutions to which we entrust the care of the elderly, has also been recognized as a real and frightening phenomenon. Maybe postpartum depression is the next painful personal problem we must address urgently and honestly. Baby food and formula ads notwithstanding, we need to get real about what childbirth takes out of new mothers.

I don't mean that we need to panic about the hormone-induced "baby blues" that virtually all new moms experience about the third day after giving birth (although we do need to stop treating these young mothers as though they're cute when they're sad). But we do need to recognize the spirit-crushing, mind-numbing, can't-go-on-with-it collapse that some women feel when suddenly their autonomy is gone, their mobility is compromised, and their very identity is deep in crisis. No one who hasn't given birth can know the kind of fatigue new mothers feel, no matter how joyous they are; the tension that overtakes every fiber of their being; the angst and worry and guilt we all feel when we undertake this awesome job for which we have no real training.

My children were spaced more than three years apart. The older one was verbal, potty trained, and in preschool when her brother came along. And still I could barely get up in the morning to slog through my day of "shove it in one end, clean it up at the other." I would have given anything to shave my legs in peace, to read a book, to not clean up one more pureed carrot, to sleep soundly through the night. And I had lots of help and support. I simply cannot imagine how Andrea Yates faced having five little children under the age of 7. (Nor can I imagine that she continued to become pregnant, that her husband and others did not recognize the danger signs, that the people around her left her alone with the children with virtually no respite.)

My heart goes out to every mother who struggles with her own set of circumstances and feelings when she has a new baby. As horrible as it is to contemplate a mother killing her own children, and as sad as it is to learn of a postpartum suicide, none of us is in a position to judge that woman's actions. The most we can do is offer our compassion. Because if truth be told, inside the heart of almost every new mother lurks a potential Medea, who probably couldn't stop herself from committing such an incomprehensible act and who, in all likelihood, suffered beyond anything we mortals can imagine.

THE PAUSE THAT DOESN'T REFRESH

This time I think the sky really is falling. Or being pulled down by the half who don't hold it up.

Just in the last few days I've learned about four men in our town—all forty-something—who have left their significant others. (Two of them are twin brothers whose father pulled the same stunt during his own mid-life crisis. Could it be genetic?) One of them found a 23-year-old to soothe his angst. Another went to music camp for three weeks, fell madly in love with a woman there, and came back to tell his partner of seven years that she was history. Such is the power of singing sex.

All these guys, it seems, had been struggling with their issues for some time, centered mainly around their professional lives and identities. Sound familiar? Still, how many women find immediate refuge in the young and melodious? It happens, I'm sure, but generally we are more apt to "pass go" and run directly to therapy (rather than lawyers), confess our inadequacies, work on it, and stick it out if only for the sake of the kids. Why can't these fellas just beat a few drums and get on with life?

One of the wives in this community debacle, a bright, beautiful, wonderful woman, said in a moment of insight, "It's a wonderful anesthesia when your life isn't all that you'd like it to be and you don't want to work through your pain." In a lighter moment, she said, "If it weren't so sad, it would be downright funny." It is textbook typical.

My own reaction, since one couple are my good friends, is sober. I feel angry, sad, and betrayed. I am angry because it's bad enough when bulbous-bellied, balding jerks demand that women be svelt and sexy unto eternity, but where do they come off labeling women as irrational, impulsive, emotional, dependent, and chronically depressed? I feel sad because I love the people involved and my heart is breaking for my (female) friend's pain. And I feel betrayed because I honestly thought that my (male) friend was a *mensch*, a sensitive, kind, intelligent man who could be trusted not to hurt the people he loves. Silly me. Instead, I find out that he is just another dumb dude with the feelings of a flea. What must his son (from a first marriage) think of him as a role model? What message is he sending to his teenage daughter about men? Why couldn't he come home and say, "I'm in a crisis; can we talk?" How does seven years of "I love you" become "I've met someone" in three weeks?

The woman in this scenario is coping admirably. Her female friends have closed ranks around her, and with their care, she is beginning to eat and sleep again, to regain her sense of self, to know that she did nothing wrong and did not deserve to be treated this way. She is a smart, savvy, sensible, wonderful person. She will move on.

He, on the other hand, will probably come to his senses one of these days, but it will be too late. The family these two had formed will have been forever disrupted. She will have found her place elsewhere. His children will have forgiven him, but I suspect the bad taste in their mouth will have lingered. His friends will invite him to events, perhaps even the same events to which she comes, but it will be awkward. The sadness will have slid into memory, but it will be remembered.

All this for what? A moment of MENopause? Men! Oh, pause! And, in the vernacular of today, give me a break! Grow up! Get a life! Get real!

And don't ever tell me that women are fickle. *La Donne Mobile?* Maybe. But as Helen Rowland knows, "A man never quite gets over the idea that he is a thing of beauty and a boy forever." Or in the immortal words of Zsa Zsa Gabor, "Macho does not prove mucho."

INTERNATIONAL WOMEN'S DAY, 2002

This seems like a good time to reflect on the idea that "sisterhood is global," as feminist writer Robin Morgan noted in the title of her famous collection. Sisterhood is also globalization, I came to realize while reading Thomas L. Friedman's fine book *The Lexus and the Olive Tree*.

I had to smile reading Friedman's opening chapter in which he explains that ubiquitous term—globalization. Women knew it all along, I thought. Why doesn't anyone ever listen to us?

Friedman states that integration is the "one overarching feature" of globalization. Guess what? Women have been living integrated lives all along, and advocating for integrated approaches to how we all "do life" ever since the Women in Development movement began in 1970. We've always understood full well that women don't live their lives in nifty little compartments labeled Work, Community, Family, Home, Health, and so on. We begged for family planning programs that incorporated literacy training and girls' education, microcredit, and skill building through the appropriate transfer of technology (if women were doing all the farming in Africa, why did all the technology training go to men?). Watch any so-called Third World woman selling her wares at market with a baby strapped to her back while she mends clothes, and you will see what experts women are at integration.

Friedman also claims that "globalization has its own dominant culture." Excuse me, fellas, but we know all about dominant cultures too, and we understand all too well that we aren't one. "Globalization has its own defining structure of power," claims the erudite Mr. F. So does life for most women, and historically, that power structure has been decidedly male, especially in more conservative and less developed countries.

Finally, Friedman makes a case for innovation, relationships, and balance between individuals and the state as earmarks of globalization. Bravo, Thomas, you pass Women's Studies 101 with flying colors. Who could possibly claim to be more innovative than women, stewards of the family, the community, the environment, and more? Again, observe any Third World woman "making do" with whatever materials are available, whether it is to feed her family, to keep them clothed, or to ensure that they receive a modicum of education. Watch a rural African mama figure out how to grow vegetables in an arid environment, or an Asian woman rig up an improvised stove for cooking, or a Latina sister increase her yield in a factory, and you will see innovation personified. And when it comes to building relationships, don't ask. Everyone knows that women are expert at staying connected, a mystical talent for which they are frequently taunted and trivialized. Of course, when it comes to balancing acts, whether between individuals and government or between the needs of husbands, kids, and ourselves, no one knows better than women how vitally important, and difficult, such equilibrium can be to achieve. We spend our entire lives trying to "go there." Most of the time, no one notices.

So while I'm pleased to have Mr. Friedman explain globalization to me in easily understood terms, I would like to suggest, with the greatest respect, that we women have already "been there, done that" to a large degree. I realize, of course, that there's more to it than the few points I have chosen to highlight here—markets and trade, technology and finance, and all that good stuff. Still, it's satisfying to know that the world's women won't be bowled over by the lexicon of the 21st century. And it's especially nice to think that the world's dominant culture just might be catching up after all.

FINDING OUR VOICE IN THE VOID

The most encouraging piece of news to come out of Israel since the latest Mideast conflagration began 18 months ago is that several hundred soldiers have refused to serve in occupied Arab territory, and 10,000 Israelis have marched in support of their insubordination. Could it be that sanity may yet prevail?

Such resistance to the cruel and senseless regime of Ariel Sharon is reminiscent of our own Vietnam era. Only when massive public acts of outrage were mounted were we able to put an end to the insanity of that incursion. Now, only when Jews everywhere speak out against Israel's aggressive policies toward its Arab neighbors will there be an end to continuing atrocities on both sides in that part of this too fragile world.

As an American Jew, I know all too well that what I am saying here will be considered blasphemous by many who share my cultural history. But surely American Jews must begin to raise their voices in concerned opposition to what is happening and to acknowledge that Israel is engaging in state-sponsored terrorism; otherwise, what separates us from that which we have fled since our history began to be recorded? As I write this essay, our sacred holiday of Passover will soon begin, marking our own exodus out of Egypt. Should we not then remember our own oppression, and bring our history as a people to bear upon current events?

Make no mistake here: I know people whose family members were lost or permanently scarred in the Holocaust. I have been discriminated against as a Jew, even in the U.S. I have been to Israel and felt the threat of hostility that surrounds that extraordinary country. I listened with all the empathy a mother can bring to bear when women said to me, "You don't know what it's like having a child in the military, waiting for that knock on the door in the middle of the night."

But I have also seen the grief in an Arab mother's eyes. I have stood with the Women in Black—a coalition of courageous Israeli and Arab women who week after week stand together in solidarity on Israeli street corners to protest the death of every child affected by the Intifada and Israel's violence. Condemned by the Religious Right and other Zionists as well as by Arab reactionaries, abused in frightening ways, they stand, because they know that neither people, and none of the children, has a future without an end to the madness.

Very few Americans understand, I fear, the reality of Israel's policies and behavior toward the Arab people, and the consequences. Here are just a few examples. Arabs are frequently barred from moving outside their villages without Israeli permission. This can deprive them of their livelihood if they cannot travel to work. It may also mean that youngsters cannot attend school; women may be unable to secure basic goods. When they can move about, they must have identification papers and are subjected to random interrogations. Their every move is suspect, and like blacks in America before the Civil Rights Act, they are discriminated against every day in numerous humiliating ways. Abject poverty prevails. Air strikes and raids are an ever-present threat; war planes frequently pound Palestinian targets, often killing innocent children and others. Their leader has been placed under house arrest, their police stations bombed. Yet Israel demands that this leader and his police force put an end to violence. How shall they do that, when all the necessary resources are hammered and restricted? (As Mr. Arafat has pointed out, even the Americans weren't able to stop Timothy McVeigh or the numerous perpetrators of 9-11.) And what happens to people psychologically in such a violent atmosphere? What hope do young people have when poverty, repression, fear, and rage are all they know?

Of course, some Arabs have sworn to destroy Israel and all Jews. Innocent people are massacred in Israel every day. We all know perfectly well the roots of this bilateral animosity and the tribalism that drives it. (Thomas Friedman's book *From Beirut to Jerusalem* provides a clear history of the promised land.) The feelings of both sides are understandable and heartbreaking. Their differences may well be irreconcilable in the present climate of negotiation. But enough of scorekeeping about which side killed how many innocents today. Enough of post-World War II justifications for continuous, faceless murder. Enough of talk shows with ivory-tower politicians and scholars blabbering on about the crisis in esoteric terms. Time now to see the faces of the massacred innocents, to hear the wails of the mourning mothers, to give the gift of life, not hate, to the young.

Mr. Arafat may not be the optimum leader of the Arabs any longer. Mr. Sharon, who has done more to kill the peace process than anyone else in recent history, is clearly behaving like a villainous zealot. Perhaps Jerusalem must be divided and the occupied lands returned. But I am one American Jew who just doesn't want to hear it anymore. What I do long to hear is the laughter of children from Gaza to the Golan Heights, wisdom and compromise from voices modeled on Sadat and Rabin, and most of all, the outrage of Jews everywhere. The time has come. In the name of all humanity, enough is enough! Let the sounds of Shalom be heard from all peoples, and the blood of the lamb be upon all our doors. May our prayers for peace finally and truly be answered.

As my grandmother would have said, "From your mouth to God's ear." Inshallah.

THE FEMALE FACE OF PHILANTHROPY

Around the world today, women are applying their collective vision to the traditionally male field of philanthropy as never before. Their sense of what it means to be a philanthropist is innovative and strategic, and their personal stories are beginning to transform public policy. Social change is key as women move away from deficiency models of passive grant seeking to power-based, progressive action.

The Sociedad Mexicana Pro Derechos de la Mujer (Mexican Society for the Rights of Women), or Semillas (Seeds), as it has come to be called, is a perfect example. Founded in 1990 by Mexican feminists with support from the California-based Global Fund for Women, Semillas distributed over $150,000 to 21 organizations throughout Mexico last year. Their work has helped to build a culture of cooperation throughout Mexico. "We are about social change," says Semillas executive director Emilienne de Leon. "We are building a systematic network that can change the idea of philanthropy so that it is more cooperative and proactive." The model for social change through

211

philanthropy that Semillas envisions is one in which people are connected to each other regardless of traditional barriers. The challenge, she says, is helping donors to understand that you don't have to tell people how to do something. "It is not about building more shelters. It's about changing the system in ways that are equitable."

Bisi Adeleye Fayemi, founder and director of the African Women's Development Fund in Ghana, agrees. "There is no denying women as a powerful social force. Women are clear about their issues, actions, and strategies." The African Women's Development Fund, launched in 2000, awarded its first grants to 35 organizations across Africa last September. Similarly, in Nepal, a national women's fund was founded in 1996 to empower women economically, thereby fostering their independence. TEWA, as it is called, made 120 grants and dispersed $40,000 last year. Like her counterparts elsewhere, TEWA director Kanchan Rana knows that "power and control over resources are universal issues."

Women like these have joined together with women of the Northern industrialized countries to engage in a dialogue that shares ideas, experiences, and strategies. The Vermont Women's Fund is one example among several New England-based women's funds that speak particularly to the needs of rural women. A grant-making organization that supports the advancement, self-sufficiency, and economic and social equality of Vermont's women and girls, the Vermont Women's Fund, founded in 1994, awarded 55 grants totaling $166,400 in its first four years. It's endowment goal of $3 million is well under way, an amazing accomplishment for such a young fund.

With less than 5 percent of national foundation dollars earmarked for women and girls, the Vermont Women's Fund, like other women's funds in cities and states around the U.S., plays a vital role in helping women and girls move out of poverty, establish safe relationships, choose healthy behaviors, build communication skills, master nontraditional occupations, and strengthen their physical, emotional, and intellectual well-being.

Still, the need is enormous, and predictably, it is women everywhere who are swinging into action for an "about-face" that will make a true difference.

COOKS, CRONES, AND CHRISTMAS

In this season of festive foods, I've been thinking about how women have always coped with the culinary demands of the holidays. If you contemplate this in Jungian terms, it's been an interesting archetypal journey. Consider that women live life in three stages: As *maidens* we are youthfully eager, as *mothers* we nurture, and as *crones* we mature into wise and knowing elders. In order to fully understand this metamorphosis, you need only examine the eating habits and food preparation of women now in their 50s or older.

As post-maiden young marrieds in the 1970s, we all had our *Joy Of Cooking* at the ready and proudly produced tuna casseroles 360 new ways, the remaining five days of the year being Hamburger Helper days. Campbell soups made gourmets of us all, as we whipped up cream of mushroom or tomato sauces and shrimp molds at the holidays. With the aid of electric frying pans, Crock-Pots, and blenders, we could create elaborate dinner parties, where we traded recipes for cheese balls and watermelon baskets filled with assorted fruit goodies. There was nothing you couldn't make festive with Jell-O, Cool Whip, and a fondue pot in the days of Tupperware and Trader Vic's Polynesian sundowners. We worked hard at our culinary talents then, trying to be the "total woman" touted by Gloria Steinem's nemesis Phyllis Schlafly.

As mothers, we found we had less time for cooking. Our talents turned to decorating birthday cakes in the shape of bunnies, butterflies, and clowns. While we still tried to be pseudo-gourmets when our husbands came home at night, we yielded to Spaghetti-Os, endless peanut butter and jelly sandwiches, and trips to McDonald's for the kids as our own need for personhood grew. Then we began to open more cans and to rely on frozen foods, until TV dinners made Lean Cuisine seem positively upscale. During the Christmas season, we rolled up our sleeves and baked cookies or tried to muster our former delight in dishing up Creme de la Something, but for the most part, our tuna casseroles yielded to tuna melts, hamburger specialties deteriorated into sloppy joes, and homemade spaghetti sauce gave way to jars of anything that was thick and red. We found less time to consult Julia Child, and while Saran Wrap was in, Phyllis Schlafly was definitely out. Some of us even yielded to the growing popularity of pizza delivery. We coveted yogurt makers, popcorn poppers, individual servings of everything— anything that would make our lives less harried.

As the kids grew up, Jenny Craig became our maven. We found ourselves moving from yogurt to yoga, from Jell-O to jogging, from power snacks to power walks, from working to working out. Low-fat, no-fat, organic, and health foods were now in, with occasional splurges on ethnic dining to keep ourselves interesting. Singapore slings gave over to Bud Lite and chilled white. Bottled water, granola, fiber, and salad bars were our mainstays, although we did cheat in December. Then along came Dean Ornish (no fats) and the Atkins diet (no carbs), mad cows (no meat) and MSG (no Chinese takeout), and mercury in swordfish—as if we didn't have enough to worry about—until one day we realized we'd come full circle, advocating that natural foods in moderation were far better for us than all the adulterated, modulated, radiated stuff that tastes like plastic. Our turkeys were now organic, our cranberries fresh, and our sweet potatoes missing the marshmallows.

With the wisdom of croning, we can now look back and see that we have journeyed far: from hibachis to Webers to gas grills, from toasters to toaster ovens to microwaves, from biscuits to biscotti, from nouvelle cuisine back to basics, from no ice cream to soft ice cream (and the occasional Hagen Das), from upscale food emporia to organic farmers, from Starbucks to herbal teas, from quiche to corn bread, from martinis to microbrews. Armed with our woks and our steamers, our juicers and breadmakers, our Moosehead vegetarian cookbooks, our wooden breadboards, our bagel slicers and Cuisinarts, and our secret ways of knowing about a pinch of this and a dash of that, we whip up healthy, hearty, holiday meals faster than you can say "cappuccino." Because the fact is, while maidens and mothers are special, it takes a crone to be a true cook, at Christmas or any time of year.

MOMMY, MAY I?

There have been several of them now. They are all single friends with solid careers, and each of them hovers around the 40-year milestone. They all deeply want a child, and they are all seriously considering insemination or adoption.

That they all deeply want a child is not to say that they are desperate to have one. This is not only about their biological clocks, or their maternal instincts, or any other aspect of wanting a child that can seem to trivialize the passion with which we are driven to experience that unique bond. In fact, this is not about them at all. It is about the reactions they encounter from other women when they share the secret decision they are grappling with.

To a one, they tell me, married women with parenting partners have this reaction: "You'd have to be out of your mind!" Single mothers, especially those who have themselves adopted or have been a biological parent by choice, unanimously agree that despite the hardships and challenge, it was the best thing they've ever done.

This strikes me as a fairly extraordinary phenomenon. Since I am one of the married moms who react in the you-have-to-be-nuts mode (but I'd love to be your birth coach),

I began to wonder why we do that. I came up with a pretty troubling hypothesis.

Could it be that we feel so inadequate about our own parenting that we become hostile to any woman who actually thinks she can do it on her own? Do we resent her strength and resilience, her selflessness, her nurturing nature to such an extent that we would sabotage rather than support her?

If so, I don't think we need to be ashamed of it. Such a reaction is not as base as it seems at first. Who, after all, taught us anything about parenting—its pitfalls or its pleasures? Most of us learned the realities of motherhood from those cherubs who had the great misfortune to be our firstborn. It comes as little surprise that our worst parental conflicts are with them. It's our practice run, a time when we try to juggle our own needs with their never-ending demands.

Perhaps that is the difference for those women contemplating single motherhood at the twilight of their reproductive years. For them, the balance may have shifted. Maybe the needs of a would-be mom spill into, and include, the demands of progeny. It's quite possible that maturity brings with it the ability to absorb the dependence of childhood like a sponge soaking up spilled milk. And unconditional love, even when you can't imagine where child care, let alone college tuition, will come from.

Whatever the motivational dynamics, a mom is a mom. Those of us who've been there, partnered or not, know the importance of a shoulder to lean on during those bleak days of lost blankies and peanut butter walls. When women decide to go it alone, they need all the help they can get. And what better resource than a friend who's been there, solo or otherwise?

I've learned a lot from my friends who are contemplating single parenthood, including a few things about myself I didn't like. Now, if they call on me, I hope I'm ready, with parental guidance, a pacifier, or whatever else may be needed.

Hey, Mom, whatever works.

FAIR PLAY:
GIVING WOMEN EQUAL TIME IN THE MEDIA

Ever wonder what the news might be like if women were the majority of producers, editors, or newspaper owners? My bet is we'd see far less of the kind of images we saw ad nauseam after September 11, 2001: airplanes exploding into the twin towers of the World Trade Center, Pentagon types pontificating on military retaliation, and the occasional picture of pathos for human interest. Why? Because there is a huge gender gap in how women and men view social and political issues, and right now, those issues are filtered through a primarily white, male, corporate, North American lens, which still sidelines women and others perceived to be on the margin.

Veteran journalist Martha Gelhorn understood this reality and knew how to beat it. A reporter from the 1937 Spanish civil war all the way through the Vietnam era, she had this to say when asked to reflect on her amazing career: "I never knew any men reporters who went near a hospital, and I was a great frequenter of hospitals because that's where you really see the price of war . . . when I was stopped by guards, I just said 'I'm doing the women's angle.' It seemed so innocuous, nobody bothered me again."

Other women journalists can relate. At a forum honoring Gelhorn a few years ago, media women spoke out. One British producer said that anything arousing emotion is suspect. Human interest and hard news are seen as polar opposites by male editors, whereas women tend to see dry political or economic stories that omit the human-interest angle as spineless. "If women are working on a story, the automatic suspicion is that they are going for the soft underbelly of that story, and that [they will] come back in a ragged, emotional state, unable to cope with the rigors of professional journalistic standards," one news writer said. An editor told this anecdote: "We sent an all-male team to do a story on land mines. They found soldiers blowing up land mines, saying this is the greatest thing in the world. There were lots of explosions. But there was no woman who said, 'I'm afraid to let my children go out to play.' No teacher who said, 'I have a classroom full of kids that have no legs.' Nothing except bang-bang."

When Judy Mann retired last year after 28 years as a feminist columnist for the *Washington Post*, she titled her final column "A Farewell Wish: That Women Will Be Heard." Mann, the first journalist to use the term "gender gap" in the press, reflected that "a society in which women are invisible in the media is one in which they are invisible, period . . . . Women are a majority in the United States . . . we should be allowed to bring what interests us—as women, wives, mothers—to the table, and I don't mean token stories about child care. I mean taking apart the federal budget and seeing if it is benefiting families or the munitions millionaires."

The word on the street post 9-11 is that there is no gender gap when it comes to fighting the "war on terrorism."

Wrong again, fellas. According to several polls, including those undertaken by Fairness and Accuracy in the Media and Gallup for CNN/*USA Today*, women take a more conditional approach to fighting back They are more likely to advocate legal, nonmilitary responses to crimes against humanity—that is, if anybody thinks to ask them. Those who don't wait to be asked, and who have access to major media, like Susan Sontag, often find themselves pilloried for alternative points of view. When Sontag suggested in the *New Yorker* that U.S. foreign policy might have contributed to the vicious anti-Americanism symbolized by the Taliban, *Newsweek* blasted her in a column titled "Blame America at Your Peril." How easily a headline writer can distort or deride another perspective!

And how easily an editor can ignore a story until it suits. Media moguls were only too quick to seize on the burkha as a symbol of Taliban cruelty when Afghan women were finally free to remove it. But why, since 1995, had they failed to report on the violence and sexual assault committed against Afghan women every day, as women's advocates begged them to do?

We might also ask why so few female experts are interviewed. A nonpartisan study released by the White House Project revealed that women were a mere 11 percent of all guests on five major Sunday morning talk shows from January to June 2000. That number fell to 9 percent for the six weeks after September 11. In the print media, men wrote 92 percent of the more than 300 bylined opinion editorials that appeared in three major dailies in the month after the September attacks.

Eleanor Roosevelt was one of the few people who understood the difference it makes when female reporters are allowed "in." She would speak only to them at her press conferences in the 1930s, thereby ensuring that they were employed. Fifty years later, women were still suing newspapers and TV networks to end discriminatory hiring and promotion practices. Today, the mainstream media have admitted a few, mostly right-leaning women (think Peggy Noonan or Mary Matalin), but progressive, feminist writers like Barbara Ehrenreich (and myself) are most often relegated to small or alternative presses. Surely it's time, as analyst Jennifer Pozner has said, to move beyond journalism's most entrenched convention: that news is what the powerful say and do, not what the public experiences. When less than 15 percent of radio and TV general managers, news executives, and corporate board members in media companies are women, can we not agree that something is wrong?

Isn't it time for Judy Mann's farewell wish to finally become reality?

SACRIFICIAL SILENCE

I've been trying to figure out how to react to the recent crisis in the Catholic Church without sounding like an over-the-top angry woman. But heck, I am over-the-top angry—as a feminist, a mother, a community member, a political activist, a member of the human race. So here goes.

I'm angry as a feminist for all the obvious reasons: How dare a fraternity of so-called celibate men in black skirts tell women how to conduct their private and sexual lives! How dare they scare the bejesus out of little girls for normal feelings of self-discovery and out of adolescents for developmentally appropriate longings! And how dare they pontificate on the intellectual weakness and religious inferiority of women, deemed lesser beings and thus not permitted to hold the highest offices or to officiate at the highest celebrations of the church!

I'm furious as a mother on behalf of all the children whose trust has been betrayed and whose bodies have been abused.

I'm outraged as a political activist. How could the attorney for defrocked Boston priest John Geoghan, convicted of gross sexual abuse, argue that charges should be dropped because of a statute of limitations? And how could Cardinal Law et al. keep on covering up and moving priests around as if their crimes and misdemeanors were no more than a bad play in a chess match? "I'm sure a lot of churches are wondering how you deal with this in a proactive way," one priest said. Gimme a break!

Let me tell you about a former student of mine. Abused by a priest (as his older brother had been) when he was a young boy, he became a priest with one objective in mind: to reform the church so that it could once again be the trusted institution of faith it was intended to be. He began what he thought would be a brief and cathartic enterprise—to "out" the members of clergy that he and his friends knew from personal experience to be sexual predators. That work has never stopped. Now the head of a Chicago-based organization he founded called Link-Up, he has established a database of sexually abusive priests and nuns with documented case histories that would knock the socks off any of us. He also provides counseling services for people who share the experience of being abused by their church leaders. The case stories he is privy to are ugly, shocking, and brutally disturbing, and they just keep rolling in.

Abuse, lying, and sexual activity by the clergy are, of course, nothing new. We all remember history lessons about folks like the Medicis, not to mention Martin Luther, and we've seen the paintings of Madonna and Child in which models were frequently the paramours and illegitimate children of cardinals and popes. But that was then and this is now. Surely things have changed, we thought. Silly us.

At the end of the day, no matter how much I rant and rave on this issue, the more I am rendered speechless. What is left to say about the frightening and imperfect world in which we live, except that you really can't trust anyone anymore? What must this colossal betrayal be like for people of faith, who believed in their religious leaders' teachings and tried to live lives of virtue? What do you tell the children?

I don't know the answers. But this much I do know: The next time a man of the cloth tells one of my sisters, or any of our children, that she isn't good enough to offer communion, that her sexual behavior calls for a Hail Mary, that she should turn the other cheek, that she should be ashamed or guilty, I will, at the very least, hand the man in black a stone and suggest that he be the first to cast it. Then I will probably suggest that he go over the top, and just keep going, because God only knows what I'd do if I got my hands on him.

ABOVE ALL, DO NO HARM

Nearly 25 years ago, when I was program director of the National Women's Health Network in Washington, DC, some of the biggest issues we faced were coerced sterilization, informed consent, and drug safety and efficacy. All these important health care issues are once again in the news, reminding me that the more things change, the more they stay the same.

Governor Mark Warner of Virginia has apologized to the thousands of people, mostly women, who were sterilized without their consent in that state between 1924 and 1979, when eugenic laws ran rampant. But Virginia wasn't alone. More than half the states in the country—30, to be precise—had eugenic sterilization laws, and over 63,000 sterilizations were performed during those years. Forced sterility was sanctioned because of out-of-wedlock births, because somebody decided that someone else was "feebleminded," and sometimes to cover up rape.

Our national shame doesn't stop there. Under the rubric of "development assistance," women in some developing countries have been coerced into temporary or permanent sterilization. In refugee camps in Thailand, for example, some women could not claim their food rations without submitting to Depo-Provera injections, a contraceptive that is longlasting, irreversible, and often problem ridden. (Many women lined up for two or three shots so that their children could eat well.) Women in India were given clean saris if they would undergo tubal ligation. In America, women were often asked to sign sterilization consent forms during the throes of a long labor, or immediately after a cesarean section. Many of them were non-English speakers who couldn't read the forms thrust at them. Ironically, however, in a notorious violation of human rights, when the birth control pill was tested on unknowing, poor Puerto Rican women in the early 1960s, those given placebo drugs were denied abortions when they became pregnant.

Informed consent is also relevant in the case of drug therapies. While birth control pills were being handed out like vitamins in the 1960s and 1970s, studies were inconclusive at best about their risks and side effects. Studies conducted on beagle dogs at the time revealed a troubling incidence of breast tumors, for instance, while drug companies vigorously defended their products. Thalidomide, European women were told, was perfectly harmless. Supposedly, so were diethylstilbestrol or DES and Bendectin, the former for "sealing" a pregnancy when miscarriage threatened, the latter for aiding in morning sickness. But like thalidomide, those drugs turned out to be highly teratogenic, causing enormous harm in utero.

More recently, hormone replacement therapy (HRT) has been touted as the answer to heart disease, Alzheimer's disease, and osteoporosis in women. HRT, like the birth control pill, has been routinely prescribed with little to no individual risk assessment, let alone attendance to consumer preference. Trust-me-and-take-it has been the physicians' clarion call. Now comes evidence that neither heart disease nor Alzheimer's is offset by HRT. In fact, HRT might even increase a woman's chance of having a heart attack. Yet last year, the HRT Premarin was the third most prescribed drug in America.

More generically worrying is the recent revelation that the Food and Drug Administration (FDA) is approving a number of drugs—one in five, actually—that create serious problems after being taken for a period of time. According to the FDA itself, nearly 20 percent of new drugs receive update warnings or are withdrawn from the market after gaining government approval, perhaps because of the trend to approve new drugs in a shorter time.

One health care advocate calls current drug prescribing "Russian roulette," a less than reassuring label for anyone just prescribed the hottest thing on the market. It's even less reassuring to learn that in addition to being bombarded by pharmaceutical advertising and pressure from detail personnel, doctors often aren't reading package inserts or the latest *PDR (Physician's Desk Reference)*.

The FDA is trying to quell fears by saying that the Harvard Medical School study that revealed these problems was "overstated." Of course, with all scientific research there are caveats, and in all medical practice there are extenuating circumstances. Still, 16 drugs have been recalled after being on the market for two years as a result of the study—not exactly promising.

Lessons of the past, and the present, are important for health care consumers, as well as for their practitioners, and the simplest of these lessons is the oldest and probably the most sound: Do no harm. For those of us long involved with the women's health movement, the wisdom of those three little words has been our raison d'etre. Would that we no longer had to struggle for them to be honored.

A WHISTLE-BLOWER WHO GOT LUCKY

FBI agent Coleen Rowley is one of the lucky ones. She told the truth about her workplace and survived—with a little help from Senator Chuck Grassley (R-Iowa), who pressed FBI Director Robert Mueller to guarantee that Rowley would not be punished for having criticized her employer. Rowley is the Minneapolis agent who sent a scathing letter to Mr. Mueller alleging serious shortcomings in the FBI. It was her May 21,2001 letter accusing FBI headquarters of blocking an aggressive investigation of terrorist suspect Zacarias Moussaoui that launched congressional hearings into possible intelligence failures that may have contributed to the successful terrorist attacks on the World Trade Center. Rowley called the FBI a bureaucracy rife with "risk aversion," "roadblocks" to investigations and "endless, needless paperwork."

Most women whistle-blowers are not so lucky. They tend to get blown away themselves when they reveal problems at work. Dr. Suzanne Hadley is a case in point. Several years ago, when the scientific community was debating the question of who really deserved credit for isolating the HIV virus, Hadley was a scientist working at the National Institutes of Health Office of Scientific Integrity. When, at the request of a superior, she declined to rewrite a report about a noted researcher at NIH that would have slanted the argument in his favor, she began to experience serious harassment. Her telephone records were investigated, she was barred from meetings, and later demoted amidst accusations of "lack of objectivity." After a hideous set of circumstances in which she was repeatedly persecuted at work, she resigned.

Karen Pitts and Jackie Brever provide another example. They are two women who simply told the truth when the FBI was investigating their employer, the Rocky Flats plutonium plant in Colorado. Because they answered questions about safety issues at the plant, they were both subjected to vandalism, sexual harassment, and death threats. They too ultimately resigned, and neither could find work again in their small community, which saw them as "high risk" local versions of noted whistle-blower Karen Silkwood.

These are only two illustrative examples from myriad stories and they go back several years. But things haven't changed much. Women, and many men, who tell the truth about where they work are almost without exception severely punished. However women suffer added burdens. Generally marginalized in the workplace to begin with, women who raise questions about cost, policy, ethics, safety, or legalities tend to be harassed more quickly than men because they are already outside the power structure. They are more likely to be labeled "crazy" and to be forced into psychotherapy as a condition of keeping their jobs. They are more readily accused of being "bad for morale." And women whistle-blowers are almost always tagged forever as troublemakers with an attitude. One woman who was fired (and later exonerated) after 28 years of service said, "You try to do the right thing, and then management says you have an attitude problem."

A Washington, DC, attorney who specializes in defending whistle-blowers, has said that "in 99 percent of cases you're going to be destroyed. That's the reality of the American workplace." She points out that while whistle-blowers serve society as "agents of accountability" it is very difficult to protect them. She and other advocates for whistle-blowers advise women, among other things, to "know what you are getting into" before letting a sense of morality overrule caution because women often don't have the financial resources or support systems that men do. Advocates also advise women to assess the situation they face realistically. Many women have lost their families, their friends, and their sense of community and personal safety in addition to their jobs once they embarked on a truth-telling mission. "At the very least," says one professional, "you will be viewed as disgruntled, and as someone who can't hold down a job." Some women have experienced such severe harassment that they end up with serious psychiatric problems, the most prevalent being depression and Post Traumatic Stress Disorder. Often the legal system can be as punishing as the workplace. That's why support groups are so essential.

Still, most women who have "been there" don't hesitate before saying they'd take the same steps again. "My behavior was correct," Karen Pitts said. "I'd do it again in a heartbeat," concurred Jackie Brever. "Maybe some day it will change. In the meantime, at least I won't be a disgrace to my gender."

Coleen Rowley was neither a disgrace to her gender nor to her profession. She did the right thing, and it has served all Americans well. "I really care about the FBI," she told reporters. "I've invested half my life in it." In applauding her risktaking behavior, Senator Grassley called Ms. Rowley a "patriotic American."

There are many other patriotic Americans in the workplace whose stories don't have such happy endings. They are the numerous women (and men) who have been driven out of their chosen careers, workers who did not have anyone on Capitol Hill watching out for their interests when things got tough. Perhaps Coleen Rowley's courage will inspire them. When it does, let's hope that the places where they work will look upon their acts as bravery, and not as dementia.

WHAT'S IN A NAME?

Shakespeare's Juliet is famous for asking, "What's in a name?" A rose, she said, was still a rose, no matter what you called it. It's a nice sentiment and makes for good copy, but I'm afraid it won't fly when applied to some of the names people (usually of the male variety) give to women.

I was reminded of the continuing struggle to help (mostly) men understand why language is so important when we visited some old friends recently. I go back 40 years with this couple; when we first met I was 17 and they were young marrieds with children. Rob is as kind and bighearted as the day is long, as the expression goes, but he is definitely retro. A product of an Old World Italian family, a former military man, and a seafarer, he is a throwback to the days when females were best kept barefoot and pregnant in the eyes of the patriarchs. So when he asked me to explain why calling women "gals" was so offensive, I started at square one, explaining power dynamics, trivialization, objectification, and a few other principles of Feminism 101.

"It's diminutive," I concluded.

"So why are guys guys?" he asked. That was a bit trickier to explain, but I think he got the generic and self-appointed nature of the term. I also pointed out that as male is to female, so man is to woman. *Woman,* I said, referred to an adult female, as *man* referred to an adult male.

"What about 'ladies'?" he asked. "What's wrong with that?"

"It has certain connotations," I suggested. "Ladies are supposed to behave, to carry themselves in a certain way. It comes with imposed expectations."

"What about gentlemen?" To his credit, he was really thinking about all these semantics. "What's wrong with 'ladies and gentlemen'?"

Nothing, as a greeting, I said. But the terms were similarly laden with value judgments for both sexes. Only they were more laden for "ladies," and certainly more frequently invoked.

I'm not sure Rob altogether got the importance of my explanation, but I certainly give him credit for trying to understand why many women resent terms that others may find endearing. Would that more men, and anti-feminists, grappled with the importance of language, which, after all, informs all of what we know, aids in our self-identity, and gives us expression.

Perhaps the most important piece is to realize that there is nothing knee-jerk in women's distaste for a nomenclature that suggests they are "smaller" or less than their male counterparts. Most women who care about the lexicon of our day understand the historical and psychological implications of various "terms of endearment" that only serve to trivialize, diminish, or set childlike expectations. Such expectations carry over beyond our daily interactions with those we know and trust. They find their way into research methodologies and analysis, into classrooms, medical facilities, military institutions, corporations, government, the marketplace—indeed, everywhere women have a too often invisible presence. Children learn all too early what is expected of them by virtue of their gender, partially through how we use language; they recognize the rewards and punishments of outdated and stereotypic roles by grade school, which is why adolescent girls hide their intellectual capacity by the time they are in their teens.

Language has an enormous impact on our lives. Little words here and there matter, even when they are used innocently and with affection. Girls can do things gals are likely not to try. (Guys are impressed). Women sweat. Ladies perspire. (Gentlemen don't notice.)

Eleanor Roosevelt once noted that "no one can make you feel inferior without your consent." That's why the mantra of many a feminist is "Don't call me Girl!" The line is not simply a polemic; it's a line in the sand, a rally for survival, the great "I am!"

I sure hope all you boys out there, big and small, can relate.

WOMEN'S MENTAL HEALTH CARE: FRAUGHT WITH PROBLEMS

When Phyllis Chesler's book *Women and Madness* first appeared in 1972, it was hailed by feminist critics for providing valuable documentation of the damage done to women by psychiatry. Chesler's work was well-researched, profoundly disturbing, and vital to the women's movement. It dramatically captured the terrifying history of errors in women's diagnosis and treatment, thereby validating women who were sensing problems with their own care and, one hopes, offering insights to practitioners providing that care.

But long before Chesler's classic book was published, women had individually recorded their frightening experiences with the mental health establishment. Many of these accounts were shared in *Women of the Asylum: Voices from Behind the Walls: 1840-1945*, by Jeffrey Geller and Maxine Harris (Anchor Books, 1994). Here is Lydia Smith describing her admission to the hospital where she spent six years: "I was plunged into a bath, the water of which was not quite boiling hot, and held down by a strong grip on my throat, until I felt a strange sensation and everything began to turn black . . . . When I became conscious I found myself being jerked from one side to the other, with my hands confined in the stocks or 'muff' . . . . and a stout leather belt attached to an iron buckle, was around me . . . . I was taken into a small division off from the main hall, and thrown into a 'crib.' The strap attached to the 'muff' was fastened to the 'crib' in such a manner as to tighten across the pit of my stomach, with such a pressure it actually seemed to me that I could not breathe." The torturous description continues with a graphic portrayal of force-feeding and forced administration of medication, resulting in five of Lydia's teeth being knocked out.

Mary Jane Ward described her 1941 meds regimen this way: "At a desk was a woman in white uniform and cap. She was serving something in lilycups . . . . One woman knocked the cup from the guard's hand, but the white uniform simply filled another cup and said, 'You drink this!'" Ward also recalled electroconvulsive therapy: "They put a wedge under your back. It forced you into an unnatural position . . . . Now the woman was putting clamps on your head, on the paste-smeared temples and here came another one, another nurse-garbed woman and she leaned on your feet as if in a minute you might rise up and strike the ceiling. Your hands tied down, your legs held down. Three against one. I opened my mouth to call for [help] and the silly woman thrust a gag into it and said, 'Thank you, dear,' and the foreign devil with the angelic smile and the beautiful voice gave a conspiratorial nod."

This year, another, more contemporary book will be published about women's experiences with the psychiatric treatment milieu, and it has been my privilege to edit it. I was first inspired to collect women's stories about their psychiatric care when I learned of a research study conducted by Wanda K. Mohr, a professor in the College of Nursing at

Rutgers University. Dr. Mohr had done a systematic comparative analysis of both Victorian and contemporary women's accounts of their hospitalizations for mental health reasons, and her findings were alarming: Virtually nothing had changed in a hundred years in terms of how women perceived, and described, their treatment and hospitalization experiences. Women today feel just as victimized, just as angry and fearful, and just as badly or maliciously treated as their 19th-century sisters. Psychiatrists and other mental health care providers seem to be just as ill-equipped, arrogant, and misogynistic in their practices as they were when Lydia Smith was committed to an asylum a century ago. Here are some excerpts from *Women's Encounters with the Mental Health Establishment: Escaping the Yellow Wallpaper* (Haworth Press, 2002):

"As I contemplate my escape, my head begins to throb with anger. The nurses deceived me when they told me they wanted my valuables for safekeeping. They knew no one could steal anything from my room. I'm being watched every second . . . . My throat tightens with disgust as I remember my naivete, my complicity in stripping myself of my freedom."

"We were all kept in the locked side of the psych unit, which consisted of a narrow hallway, a room with a table, chairs, a TV attached to the wall, and a row of sleeping rooms—small cells—each with a mattress on the floor and a video camera high on a corner of the wall."

"The psychiatrist never made eye contact, and really didn't seem interested in anything I had to say . . . . He would sit in the plastic chair, staring out the window or down at his shoes. I waited for him to begin, but he never did. After about a minute he'd sigh heavily and then he'd be gone."

"I remember all the devices to make me forget. I remember being stretched out on the table counting 10, 9, 8—held down one aide on each side. I remember screaming 'No! No!' I remember an order to increase the voltage. I remember passing out to the electrical shocks."

In the afterword to this anthology, Wanda Mohr identifies two themes in women's writing about their own treatment-seeking experiences: "Hear me, I am Person!" and "Preserve my dignity! I am a human being!" She writes, "Experiences with the mental health system can be abusive and dehumanizing . . . . Too frequently spoken and unspoken pleas are not heeded by a system that is designed to label, control, medicate, and discharge. The pronouncement comes, the diagnosis is conferred, and magically the woman patient is assigned a label that transforms from 'her' to 'it.'"

Why is it taking so long for "her" to be seen? Peter Breggin, quoted in *They Say You're Crazy* by Paula Caplan (Perseus Books, 1995), suggests that "only in psychiatry is the existence of disease determined by APA [American Psychiatric Association] presidential proclamations, by committee decisions, and even at times by a vote of the members of APA, not to mention the courts." Caplan's book offers a critical examination of the APA's *Diagnostic and Statistical Manual of Mental Disorders (DSM)*, the Bible of psychiatric diagnosis. "Today in North America," she asserts, "classifying people as normal or abnormal is a major enterprise that is carried out on many levels." Such classification, she says, is often arbitrary and based on vested interests. Caplan exposes the APA for its "claims to have produced a diagnostic system based on scientific research that will allow [them] to know what kinds of treatment will be helpful for whom." She says that such claims are unwarranted.

The Victorian era had no trained psychiatrists, no APA, no *DSM*. It would be easy to look back and judge the villainous behavior of asylums and the people who supported them in those dark times. But our own failure to progress in the sound diagnosis and humane treatment of people, particularly women, suffering despair and mental illness defies explanation, outside of a troubling political and patriarchal rationale. Perhaps that observation only serves to prove a truism: The more things change, the more they remain the same—a worrisome prognosis for any American woman in psychological crisis.

MERGERS THAT MATTER

In the interest of full disclosure I confess that I haven't actually read Sylvia Ann Hewlett's book, "Creating A Life: Professional Women and the Quest for Children." But I've read quite a bit about it, as well as lots of stuff like it. So I have to say that I'm getting pretty tired of the demands made on women to choose between love and work, and the scare tactics that force them into such unfair choices.

Hewlett's book adds to the plethora of "post feminism" offerings on the challenges of being both a female parent and a professional. It is the product of a survey she conducted that revealed that more than a third of highly paid professional women over 40 do not have children, either by choice, or because they waited too long. Critic Susan Chira duly noted in her *New York Times* book review that this fact, and the dilemma it represents, thrill anti-feminist backlashers, who thrive on pointing out that women really can't have it all (and shouldn't expect to). She also points out that an important question is being ignored: "How do ambitious women balance work, marriage and children?" My question is this: Why should "ambitious women" have to solve the problem all by themselves?

Even God, it appears, isn't perfect. It seems He forgot to install a biological clock when He created man. (Either that, or perish the thought, God has a pro-male bias.) Nevertheless, it takes two to tango as everyone knows. All kids have two parents, biologically speaking. So why do we expect only moms to pull themselves up by the bootstraps, Horatio Alger style, and make humanly almost impossible choices? Why aren't dads drawn into solving the problem in more than cerebral, and perhaps financial, ways? And why aren't the institutions we all work for taking any responsibility for how we raise our progeny, how we share the burdens of society, and how we demonstrate care and concern for our children, who are, after all, the future of that society?

No one asks men to choose between love and work, the two most fundamental human needs, according to Siggy Freud (who, in my view, did more to destroy women's psyche and parental confidence than anyone else in modern history). Why do we insist on placing this awesome burden solely on women?

The question of interpersonal and institutional responsibility in making life work for everyone is, of course, linked to other issues of our time. Think about the fact that welfare reform still doesn't address childcare adequately. Stop to wonder why prostitutes are arrested while their customers are not. Ask yourself how so many children in this country go to bed hungry night after night.

But I digress. The point I wish to make is this: There should be no "Mommy Track," only parent tracks. The mother of all mergers should not be about this company marrying that company. It should be a merger between employers and employees; one that recognizes the importance of personal and professional partnerships in all of our lives. It should foster a real life scenario in which both women and men can live life to the fullest—which by the way, yields the highest productivity in the workplace, which has been proven many times.

In such a scenario, families and children thrive. Businesses do well. Men and women find themselves less at odds. Sure, compromises still need to be made, negotiation skills honed. But in the long run, as well as the short, life keeps ticking along quite well, it seems to me—even, I might add, if the ticking we hear is the sound of someone's biological clock.

III

SEPTEMBER 11, 2001

SEPTEMBER 11, 2001

How shall we speak of it—
The black plumes of smoke
that darkened sparkling skies
like devils' cloaks, while
red fireballs exploded
madness upon the heavens,
and bodies rained down,
broken fragments of our
lost humanity.
When those two great towers
fell to earth in rubbled heaps,
what was there to say?
We mortals gasped,
disbelieving,
then covered our eyes,
lest we should look upon
such evil and be forever blind.
Cell by cell
the multitudes fell silent,
then sank into that
monument of hate,

and everywhere, we wept,
wondering where God had gone.
Then, silently, we lit candles,
and drew children to our breasts,
honoring life amidst decay.
Three thousand hearts
which beat no more,
thundered in our quiet prayers—
We longed for memory
to be so mute—
and dazed beyond repair,
we staggered forward,
tenuously, toward hope.

IT'S ONLY DEATH

What can one say in light of the tragedy that isn't a platitude, a truism, a clichè? Yet one feels compelled to speak, to add one's voice to the pain, the outrage, the shock, the grief. In the coming days, it will be this grief that dominates, as we learn the stories of those lost.

I know something about grief. In 1990, I lost my only sister, suddenly and tragically. In 1991, my baby brother died, just as suddenly and tragically. A year later, my mother passed away. My father had already died. All of them gone, three of them in as many years.

People ask me how I stood it when they had all gone, when those I had loved so much were dead, all of them gone so soon, so abruptly absent from my life. My sister died at the age of 52. She had a brain aneurysm. Eighteen months later, my husband phoned me while I was on a business trip. "Your brother is dead," he said, his voice trembling with fear of what that news would do to me. "He had an asthma attack and died." He was 45. One year later, my 86-year-old mother passed away, quietly, as I held her hand in a nursing home. My father had died on his 69th birthday in 1971. And so, at the age of 50, I became the last of my birth family to survive, an inconceivable reality much of the time, still.

Sometimes I wonder myself how I survived that nuclear winter of my orphaning. I can tell you this: It was only death. Only death, I realized, another way of being. And knowing that, a quietness came upon me, and suddenly I loved the little things—the rain and the sweet smell of its aftermath, the sky, the grass under my feet, the potted flowers on my deck, bright red and green peppers on a wooden chopping board, the onions that made me weep clean, cathartic, forgiving tears.

Now I can remember them and laugh, even while wanting more. When people ask me how I stand it with the others gone, I smile, glad for their compassion. "It's only death," I say. Sometimes the old ones, the wise ones, understand.

When my friend's husband died of cancer a few years ago at the height of his career, full of anticipation for his retirement, I was there. I was able to do little things to make him comfortable, and I was not afraid. I could sit with his wife and not feel awkward. I can do death now, because of what I know about it in those transcendent moments when I understand that it's only death, a different way of being.

People say I have a new calmness, that they've never seen me quite so content. I think I know what they mean. I have given up a certain kind of fear—not the attendant grief or dread that finality brings, but the fear of nonexistence.

The greatest thing I can wish for my children is that when it is my turn, they too will know that it is only death, a different way of being, and that in so many ways, my spirit soars around them.

And the greatest thing I can wish now for those who have lost loved ones in this most horrible of tragedies is that they may come to know that it is only death, a different way of being. May the many spirits of those who are gone soar among us all.

TURNING TOWARD
SHALOM

As I write this essay, it is two weeks since the disastrous events in New York, Washington, DC, and Pennsylvania changed our lives forever. It is also the High Holy Days for Jewish people everywhere, an eight-day period when we try yet again to inscribe peace upon our hearts. We celebrate Rosh Hashanah, the New Year; and we honor the most solemn day of our calendar, Yom Kippur, the Day of Atonement.

In this time of reflection, many things have become luminously clear to me. Most of them have been stated eloquently by others, but they are worth reiterating:

First, we must remain calm and considered in our attempts at retribution. As NPR commentator Adam Hockenberry said, this enemy knows us well. He understands the American psyche. We do not have the same grasp of his mind-set, his motivation. Therefore, we must be especially cautious in how we respond to the heinous acts of September 11. Otherwise, global conflagration is an entirely too real possibility.

As Americans, we must begin to examine why so many

peoples of the world loathe us. What has our 20th century legacy been? What have we done to foster such animosity toward the United States? Let us remember—we supported the Shah of Iran, we funded and armed the Taliban, we engaged in the Gulf War, we failed to censor Israel when it overstepped its bounds with regard to the rights of Palestinian people; in short, we cannot always claim the moral authority. More recently, we have snubbed the world by violating the Kyoto agreement, by our posturing on missile defense treaties, by disengaging from world events that affect us all. What is our responsibility as we move forward?

This is also a time to examine where we stand on the issue of civil liberties. While enhanced security is absolutely required, and nowhere more than in America's airports and planes, we must also exercise restraint and good judgment in the name of the freedom our founders envisioned for us. We must be absolutely certain we understand the ramifications of wiretaps and other invasions of privacy— our future sense of security may also depend on the care we take now in this regard.

But what weighs heavy on my mind as I reflect now upon the juxtaposition of tragedy and hope is this: There can be absolutely no room in the world for what we have come to know as backlash. There can be no room for violence, for rage so out of control that it spews forth upon our children. There can be no way that in reacting to terrorism we become terrorists ourselves.

When we look upon the faces of children too frightened to go to school, children who tell us that they are good people who didn't hurt anyone, children who have lost limbs and loved ones to terrorism, how can we doubt what our responsibility is to these children who represent our future?

Virginia Woolf said, "As a woman I have no nation. As a woman I want no nation. As a woman the world is my nation." I would like to paraphrase her words. As a woman I have no religion. As a woman I want no religion. As a woman children are my religion. Children are our hope, our progeny, our souls made big. What will our legacy to them be, fear or forgiveness? Ignorance or intelligent action? Compassion or condemnation? From Belfast to Bosnia, from Rwanda to Romania, from Jerusalem to Jeddah, look upon the faces of youth, and the answer should be clear.

In this time of Jewish prayer, we are ordered to turn toward Shalom. Peace. On that holiest of days, Yom Kippur, we are asked to ponder our sins and to find it in our hearts to forgive ourselves and others. As we atone for our all too human lapses, may we all find it in our hearts, above all else, to remember the children. For them, may we turn toward peace and, yes, compassion and forgiveness, even as we contemplate an appropriate contemporary response to terrorists.

Shalom, and may our prayers for sanity prevail.

STEAK KNIVES JUST WON'T CUT IT

If anyone had told me that my greatest insight about what happened in New York and Washington would come from *Larry King Live*, I never would have believed it. Yet, such is the case.

The day after the heinous attacks on those two American cities, King interviewed three people, whose names I failed to note, about airline security in this country. What they had to say made me sick, and angry.

All three guests were experts in airline safety and security. And all three were outraged at the breeches of security that had allowed four aircraft to be highjacked from three major East Coast airports. Each of them spoke of the failure of the government to grasp, still, the need for real 21st century security in the nation's aircraft and air terminals. Paraphrasing, here is what they said: Questions about who packed your bags and where they've been since they were packed are a joke. Stopping curbside check-in and curtailing the passing out of steak knives is a joke. Having ill-trained and poorly supervised minimum-wage workers staffing xray machines is a travesty. Security is a function of policing; it is not appropriate to have such security functions carried out by a government agency like the FAA, which still "doesn't get it." Opening airports prematurely, primarily for economic reasons, is also a travesty. And here is the most sickening part: For years, all three of these people have testified, pleaded, argued, cajoled for improved safety in the skies. According to one of King's guests, the FAA apparently thought that while it was important to give the appearance of complete security, necessary measures such as having air marshals aboard every flight were just too expensive, and the public wouldn't stand for increased fares. Just how expensive is too expensive, I wonder. Ten thousand people? Twenty thousand?

Twelve years ago, it seems, an Israeli airline security official testified before the U.S. Congress on the need for improved airline security in this country, including armed air marshals on flights. Ever wonder why no one ever tries to take out an El Al jet?

Ironically, just after the King program aired, Bush administration officials announced that they were considering putting air marshals on American flights. Timing is everything.

The psychologists were right. First there is disbelief, followed by grief, and then anger. I still can't believe what happened. I continue to grieve. But I am also angry. Furious, in fact, at the almost unbearable thought that with a little more foresight and attention to the experts, this whole wrenching, incredible series of tragic events might never have happened.

As we begin to travel the long road to recovery, I believe we must bring pressure to bear on Congress for appropriate, adequate, and timely security measures surrounding air travel. It may cost us something, but not nearly as much as failure to ensure such security, and not nearly as much as we have already paid.

THE HOMELESS, HUNGRY, TEMPEST TOSSED

As early as 431 B.C. Euripides understood: "There is no greater sorrow on earth than the loss of one's native land."

Today, the world faces a flood of sorrowful refugees beyond anything we might have imagined, and that was true even before the events of September 11 spawned an exodus from Afghanistan that now threatens to destabilize the borders of Iran and Pakistan. Afghans, like many others, also seek asylum in Britain and Australia. When the Norwegian boat carrying more than 400 of them was turned away recently from Australia and could not return to Indonesia, I tried to imagine what it was like for the people crowded onto that ship. What was it like, I wondered, when the Exodus was turned away from Palestine, when the borders of African nations were closed to families fleeing war and famine, when Indians walked to Pakistan and Pakistanis walked to India during partition, when the people of Cambodia and Vietnam fled to Thailand, when immigrants flooded Ellis Island? No one who has never been exiled can know.

But imagine what life is like in the burgeoning refugee

camps of the world. Long lines for meager rations, long rows of lean-tos and makeshift tents for living in, long days of boredom and hopelessness, in some cases barbed wire and always the barren landscape of endless waiting. And that's if you're lucky. For the unlucky, there is often violence and abuse, chronic illness, starvation and despair.

Women and children, an estimated 75 to 90 percent of the world's displaced people, often suffer most. "Despite the strength and courage that has carried them out of their homelands, refugee women have special needs in terms of shelter, supplies, and health care," says the United Nations High Commissioner for Refugees. "They also require attentive preventive action to protect them from sexual violence and exploitation at all stages of their flight."

Why in a time of such sadness should we have to think of this human disaster too? Because the numbers of refugees and internally displaced persons is growing exponentially, and no one wants them. The lady with the lamp is sagging. There is no more golden door.

Fifty years ago, after World War II, the United Nations clearly laid out the world's responsibility toward displaced peoples. More fortunate nations had an obligation, it said, to treat migrants humanely, to take their claims of persecution seriously, to offer sanctuary and protection. Human rights, it implied, were the solemn obligation of all. But no one could have imagined what the world would look like 50 years hence. Modern travel, ethnic and religious wars, brutality among "leaders," drought, disease, and famine, natural and unnatural disasters, have increased the numbers of people in need of sanctuary and protection beyond what the stable countries of the world can bear, and they are crying "Enough!" Anti-refugee laws now flourish, and asylum seekers have become a challenge, a political issue, a nemesis.

It's not hard to understand why. In 1989, for example, 4,000 people applied for asylum in Britain; last year, despite controls, there were more than 83,000 applications there.

Multiply this by all the member nations of the European Union alone, and the magnitude of the problem becomes clear. (Last year, nearly half a million people applied for asylum in Europe.) What to do?

That question is what European countries, and others, are trying to answer. Just how should they define, and honor, the 1951 UN Convention Relating to the Status of Refugees? In the meantime, the world's 12 million refugees wait, wander, and wonder how they will survive. When I contemplate this overwhelming phenomenon, I cannot fail to imagine the sick and wretched boat people clinging to life, the mothers delivering newborns in fly-infested desert tents, the children without schools and laughter, the aching hearts of the forlorn elderly, the despair of grown men who know not how they will live.

Somehow, along with everything else we must cope with in these difficult times, we cannot forget the plight of refugees and internally displaced people. The nations of the developed world must remember these seething masses "yearning to breathe free." We must devise a way, once again, to raise a light beside our doors. Not only do the lost souls of the world ask it of us. So does our own humanity.

"THE STEEL STILL PIERCES MY HEART"

The Latina woman who speaks these words is standing next to me at an extraordinary photographic exhibit in New York City. Her mother, who speaks little English, says, "This thing, it really happened? I still can't believe it." A Japanese woman, sobbing, tells me, "My son was late for work that day." We embrace. Dozens of people mill about, some tearful, some with their hands over their mouths, some clinging to the person next to them. More people wait patiently on the street to enter the exhibit. It is exactly one month since the infamous "9-11."

"Here Is New York: Images from the Frontline of History: A Democracy of Photographs" is on display in Manhattan's Soho district. The month-long display is a memorial, a catalyst, a place to honor the memory of what happened on a bright sunny morning in this vibrant city last month. It is a place to come to grips with the unfathomable, perhaps to grieve, to reconcile, to reach closure.

Central to the exhibit of several hundred professional and amateur photographs is this prophetic 1949 quote by E.

B. White, who saw in the newly emerging jet age of his time both drama and danger: "The city for the first time in its long history is destructible. A single flight of a plane can quickly end this island fantasy, burn the towers, crumble the bridges, cremate the millions. The intimation of mortality is part of New York in the sound of jets overhead."

It leaves you speechless to read it, and to see the multitude of images hung on string with clothespins. Black-and-white photos, color images, simple renditions of the twin towers, complicated collages, weeping, weary faces, fatal moments, flags, it's all there. In one indelible picture, a bald, beefy fireman cries like a baby. In another, white dust covers the detritus of September 11, 2001 as if it were a newly discovered archeological site. Then there is the photograph of chalk on the sidewalk that reads, "I am an iron worker. I held you in my hands. I did not know who you were and now I am showered and clean but yet I still feel dirty. I don't know why, but I feel ashamed. Who were you?"

In one corner of the studio, a video replays the airplanes crashing into the World Trade Center. Over and over, the unbearable image is repeated, and people crowd around to watch it yet again. I ask a man why. He says, "To help us believe it is real." Another man tells me, "They say it's the end of New York. It makes me so mad." I share with him that I am a former New Yorker, and we look at each other in the understanding that New Yorkers are not that easily defeated.

This unconventional gallery show is the brainstorm of Michael Shulan, owner of the building on Prince Street where the exhibit is being shown, Gilles Peress, a photographer for the *New Yorker*, and the Photography Department of the School of Visual Arts. It all began when Shulan put a poem and a photo in the window of his vacant storefront. Peress saw it and the attention it drew, suggested a collaboration, and the show was born. "All we did," says Shulan, "is provide a forum for people's expression. Photographs bear witness. They are a cathartic act. We are glad that people find solace here." The photos, he says, represent the mind-set of the nation, and "with today's technology, democratizing our collective experience is possible."

The unjuried photographs on display were submitted by anyone who took pictures relating to the September tragedy. Digitally scanned and printed, novice photographers' work appears alongside the work of top photojournalists. Visitors can buy a reproduction of any photograph for $25, all of which is donated to the Children's Aid Society 9-11 Fund.

In their press release, Here Is New York organizers say, "In order to restore our sense of equilibrium as a nation, and as a community of individuals, we need to develop a new way of looking at and thinking about what happened." Their innovative exhibit, which will become a traveling exhibit and a book, affords us that opportunity, even as the steel continues to pierce our hearts.

PROACTIVE PACIFISM: OXYMORON OR REALITY?

"I used to be a process person. Then I passed 50, and now I just want to know who's going to do what by when!" That's what I tell my students when they generalize and speak in lofty, abstract, and often naive terms. How are those good ideas going to be operationalized? I ask them. What exactly are you going to do to achieve your objectives, and what measurable milestones will you put in place to see if your plan is succeeding?

That's not to say that process isn't important. Like most liberals (and feminists), I am still deeply committed to the idea of creative exploration, grassroots participation, and idealized goals. But being focused on the task-oriented aspects of those goals helps to realize the purpose and objectives of any endeavor. Being able to name, and carry out, the exact steps that need to be taken to bring about social change will move the process along much faster than the most clearly articulated and impassioned rhetoric, and with the greatest respect, I suggest that the voices of opposition to America's "war on terrorism" still need to grasp this lesson.

Feminists have been extraordinary in their analysis of what is wrong with everything from welfare reform to women's place in the world order, but seldom have I heard a viable strategy for defeating patriarchy in all its ramifications. Those who oppose globalization have been brilliant in organizing and mobilizing their forces to take to the streets. But much of their rant-and-chant has been ill-informed, and most of it has lacked a cogent and realistic plan for change.

Now comes the pacificist movement that accompanies all times of war. Let me be clear: I am as against war and violence as anyone now marching, lobbying, and otherwise advocating for a peaceful resolution to the current crisis of cultures that threatens us in monumental ways unimaginable prior to September 11. If there is a way to change the world and bring our collective humanity into focus, I support it wholeheartedly.

But I have worked in the developing world for many years, and the reality of that experience makes me ask the same questions of pacifists that I ask of my students: How are we going to operationalize our goals? What specific steps can we take to ensure that terrorism disappears from the face of the earth? How exactly shall we ensure our objectives in light of some amazingly difficult realities?

For a start, the pacifist argument emanates from a rational and highly educated, intelligent framework. Uneducated pseudo-Islamic zealots are not likely to understand at all "where we are coming from." Their indoctrination is so deep and pervasive that it allows mothers to raise their eyes to the heavens and wish that all their sons may die in glory. How can we combat that level of insanity?

How do you work in a country without the invitation and cooperation of its government? Even when such invitation is forthcoming, as it has been for years when foreign assistance is sought, how do you overcome the myriad obstacles that arise from weak or absent infrastructures? How do you suddenly communicate with people and bring them goodwill as well as basic goods when there are no roads or radios and when all that matters is surviving the next day? How do you talk about fellowship and our common humanity with people who are illiterate, starving, afraid, and repressed (many of whom see America as the reason for these ills)? Beyond talking, how do you change behaviors, attitudes, knowledge, skills, cultures, whole societies in time? How do you deal with the corruption that rules in the Third World? Beyond diverting military expenditures, how do you finance such a massive objective as global social change, which at best would take generations to achieve? Who do you train in the complexities of cultures that are so foreign to the Western mind?

It is pure Pollyanna, in my view, not to take into consideration these very real and pressing issues when pushing for a more peaceful solution to the massive dilemma of our time. That is not to say that I wouldn't welcome a way to fight terrorism without becoming terrorists ourselves. Like everyone else of sound mind, I would welcome—indeed, embrace—an alternative solution to routing what President Bush insists on labeling "evil." But as a post-50 realist, I would ask that those seeking a peaceful resolution stay grounded in the reality of the times in which we live. "Killing them with kindness" makes good copy, but it has never been a viable strategy. As every ex-socialist knows, human nature just keeps getting in the way. Add to human nature poverty, power, and a people with no hope beyond a holy death, and somehow the idea of food and flower handouts just doesn't seem to stand up. But then, I'd love to be proved wrong.

THE POLITICAL IS PERSONAL

Kudos to Ellen Kaye, Robert Riversong, and Ellen David Friedman, all of whom made their voices heard recently with respect to America's newly developed war policy.

Riversong and Kaye, both of Brattleboro, wrote letters to the *Brattleboro Reformer*, while Friedman spoke out in an October 15 VPR commentary. Each of them acted upon their political convictions. Each of them took a risk to "speak truth to power." And each of them was willing to stand up and be heard, even if what they had to say was hugely unpopular. That takes real courage, especially in a time of nationalism bordering on xenophobia.

In her October 16 letter to the paper, Ellen Kaye said, "I have an obligation to speak out when harm is being perpetrated against people, regardless of the borders that superficially define them, and regardless of the identity of the perpetrator. I have the right to speak and will exercise that right even if social pressure or repressive laws attempt to forbid it."

On October 18 Robert Riversong wrote a powerful letter calling for "a vigilant and critical media and an American citizenry concerned with protecting the principles which make this nation great."

In her radio essay, Ellen David Friedman wanted "to stand up for the function of dissent." Questioning the apparent national consensus supporting the bombing of Afghanistan, she had this to say: "It feels to me as if the sheer horror and scale of the September 11 attack shut down our capacity for national dialogue . . . . We serve our democracy poorly if we act solely from raw emotions. It is our ability, instead, to examine fully, debate freely, and to agree democratically that ensures actions for which we can accept long-term responsibility."

One may not agree with all the points of view expressed by these people and others when they write letters and commentary, call talk shows, or make their views known to their congressional representatives. That doesn't matter. What does matter is that these individuals are exercising the most fundamental of rights in a democratic and free society: They are acting politically. They are engaging in the free flow of opinion that underpins and informs a democracy. They are taking seriously their solemn responsibility to participate. They are girding the pillars of the institutions we so take for granted that some of us don't even bother to vote.

There are many reasons in this time of crisis and uncertainty to "get political." For one, voices of opposition are being stifled, and that is dangerous. When talk-show hosts or newspaper editors lose their jobs for dissenting with official policy and callers are cut off or rudely condemned by ill-informed and impatient radio jocks, when pacifists are shouted down for voicing humanistic concerns and students are afraid to speak up, something is terribly wrong in a country that prides itself on First Amendment rights. When people try to understand why there is such global animosity toward America and are dismissed or labeled stupid and unpatriotic, something is wrong. When people offer new ways of thinking about how to effect justice and are laughed at as naive, something is clearly amiss.

There is also something wrong when a democratic government acts with such speed and secrecy that no one seems to know what is actually happening. National security notwithstanding, at what point do we begin to question the wisdom of withholding information? Further, what has been happening on Capitol Hill since September 11 that we don't know about? What bills are being pushed through without public debate and discourse? How much pork has passed through those hallowed portals without so much as the blink of an eye?

And what is being ignored there? Will women's issues, social services, health, and education be borrowed from and trivialized yet again, as they traditionally are in a time of "war"?

This is not a time to assume, metaphorically speaking, that one's vote doesn't matter. Every voice, every point of view, every question, idea, innovation, critique we can muster must be spoken, shared, debated. It is absolutely crucial that the sounds of democracy flourish in this time of crisis and uncertainty. As Ellen David Friedman said in her commentary, "We can't afford the luxury of silence." More than ever before, we need the sound of various voices and the chorus of pluralism ringing over our land, loud, clear, and confident that participation ensures a free and sane society.

THINK HYSTERICALLY, ACT NORMALLY

Talk about your mixed messages! The vice president is in a bunker somewhere; the Congress (in typical me-first fashion) has fled its offices; airports, post offices, and other federal buildings are crawling with dogs, armed guards, and latex-wrapped examiners; anthrax is the *A* word for the day, and George W. et al. tell us to relax, stay calm, and return to our normal routines. Rudy Guiliani tells us to do the right thing: Come to New York and spend money. Talking heads on TV admonish us not to overreact.

Rooting for Rudy, I opted for a quick visit to Manhattan, cheered on by the fact that I'd been scheduled to appear on a panel in the Big Apple for six months anyway, making it easy for me to be loyal on two fronts. Here's what my day in New York was like not too long ago as I suppressed my natural tendency toward anxiety and encouraged a somewhat dormant exuberance.

*   *   *

Having taken the Sprain Parkway into the city so that I had only one little bridge to cross, I reached my hotel, insisting to the valet that it was no trouble at all to park my own car—which I did, 10 blocks from my Penn Station hotel. Checking in, I requested a room no higher than the third floor, above which I know you cannot jump to safety. I noted the emergency exits on my floor, decided I could drink bottled water without ice, worried that the window wouldn't open, and decided to brush my teeth. I paused only for a moment as I spread the white toothpaste over the bristles of my brush to wonder how you'd actually know if anthrax had surreptitiously been introduced. I carefully spit all the rinse water out of my mouth as I have learned to do in developing countries and headed outdoors, glancing around the lobby for lurking suspicious characters. At the subway entrance, I hesitated and considered taking a bus or, better still, walking the 24 blocks to my destination, but in the interest of expediency, I decided the odds were in my favor that nothing would have infiltrated the vent system of my particular train that day. Exiting the underground, I glanced up at the skies, where nothing seemed amiss, and made my way to West 54 Street.

At the event where I was speaking, I grabbed an end seat on the dais, opened another bottled water, and smiled at the waiter who wanted to pour me a glass from a communal pitcher. As the room filled, I checked out the faces in the audience and eyed the exits, noting with comfort that all seemed well. At the closing reception, I passed on the hors d'oeuvres, wondered if alcohol and anthrax are compatible, then grabbed a glass of chilled white.

Later that evening, I headed for a theater on 44 Street, pausing to join the multitudes who, necks craned, were reading the Times Square ticker-taped news of further disasters. I marveled at all that neon, as I always do, and controlled the thought pushing its way into my consciousness: What better way to demoralize a nation than to hit the heart of what many believe to be its cultural center? Three hours and one Lion King later, followed by a meal and a Merlot, my equilibrium was restored. I returned to my hotel, flashed my room key at the security guard posted at the elevators, checked behind the shower curtain, and crawled into bed. I felt decidedly victorious. I had, after all, survived the day and, for the most part, kept my wits about me.

The next morning when I went to retrieve my car, I knew instantly that New York and I were indeed returning to normal. First, the parking attendant wouldn't honor my discount vouchers (because I hadn't driven out and back in again by four in the morning—silly me). Then I threw one major New Yorker—style fit (which I'm adept at, having lived there for three years).

As I drove up the Henry Hudson Parkway, the sun shining on the gentle waves of the river, it might have been any other Sunday in the city, I thought, as long as I kept my eyes off the rearview mirror. But for the view behind me—so naked without those twin monoliths looming over lower Manhattan—and the unusually frequent wail of sirens, things seemed pretty New York as usual. At the bridge, I handed the gloved attendant the exact toll, sipped my Perrier, and, with a sigh of relief, headed north.

GIVING THANKS FOR SIGNIFICANT OTHERS

With the events of September 11 now part of our collective unconscious and the Thanksgiving holiday before us, I've been reflecting on an important question: If someone were to ask me what I would do if I "had it to do all over again," what would my answer be? Easy. I would love my friends and relations so well that no matter what, they could love me back in the same way—without reservation, free of quid pro quos, angst, or rivalry; in short, unequivocally.

What is it, I wonder, that gets in the way of relationships between people whose connection to each other is so profound that nothing ought to be able to harm it? I began thinking about this question because of the extraordinary rifts that seem so frequent among family members. It is particularly painful for me to observe the obstacles that tear through the bonds of sisters. Has there always existed such an awful, almost inevitable hurting of each other's souls? Or are we just now owning the problem so hard to name? Has something fundamental gone out of our relational lives, making space for the hot acid of recrimination that appears to creep so readily into the crevices of our hearts?

Much has been made of the mother-daughter dyad in recent years, and of relationships between men and women. But almost no one, it seems, has explored the delicate territory of siblings, or of friendship, for that matter. If not altogether unmapped, these are tough topographies worthy of our attention. I became convinced of that when a friend told me with great sadness about a falling-out she'd had with her sister shortly before the sister's death. Soon after that, I had a tearful conversation with my favorite cousin, whose relationship with her own beloved sister had become so fragile she feared they would never be able to repair the damage done. Similar stories began to emerge with alarming frequency. "She's not there for me when I need her," someone would say. She did this, or didn't do that. "She just doesn't understand me. I love her dearly, but we can't seem to talk." "We're too competitive." "She doesn't know where I'm coming from."

All of it was familiar to me. I too had suffered the emotional split from a much-loved sister and had grieved the change in our relationship for years. It is an experience of loss that only those who have gone through it can know.

In each case, I gave them the same advice: No matter what your issues are, I said, find your way back to what binds you. No matter what it takes—hours of talking together, weeping, screaming, whatever—have it out until you get back in touch with the love, the loyalty, the special bonds you once had. Reclaim your sister (friend, child) before it's too late. If you don't, you may live to regret it. I could say this with quiet authority. I lost my sister, my only much—loved older sister, in 1990, before I could reclaim her, when it was too late. Each person I spoke to understood "where I was coming from," I think, but none has yet been able to act on my advice.

That scenario, while perhaps more dramatic between siblings or parents and children, isn't confined to family. Friendships and other meaningful relationships are destroyed every day over mundane as well as profound issues, or the inability to talk them through. One friend of mine, someone on my short list of people I could count on, told me once that an offhanded remark I'd made had so offended her that she could not accept my annual holiday invitation. I was stunned. Even if I had been unintentionally tactless, was that a reason to virtually end contact, breaking with a tradition that meant a lot to all of us? If I stopped talking to everyone I love who has ever offended me, I thought, life would be pretty lonely.

When did relationships become this cheap, this dispensable? When did we begin to give up on "working things out?" (Ever notice how young couples don't even try anymore, they just get divorced?) When did we start junk-piling the important connections in our lives and stop stockpiling the reservoirs of forgiveness and tolerance that made family and friendship work in spite of itself?

I talk to my cousin and my friends about this a lot. And every time a familiar ache roots itself in my chest, I wonder what would have happened if my sister had lived. Would we have done our screaming, weeping, and talking until we were able to hug our way back to sisterhood and the bonds of sibling connection? Will my cousin reclaim her sister before it's too late?

With all my heart, I hope so. Because they are the lucky ones. They can do it all over again. And that's an opportunity just too good to pass up in this fin de siècle time of fragile friendships, remote relatives, and hungry hearts yearning for snug, simple, and oh-so-delicious connection.

IV

REFLECTIONS

SPRING CLEANING

Every once in a while I find it necessary, or at least useful, to sort of sweep out my brain—have a catharsis not unlike the one many of us feel a compulsion to undertake when the first signs of spring appear. According to naturalists, it seems that the flora and fauna know that the new season is upon us; I know it too, because I need to air some thoughts.

The first thing cluttering my mind is my contempt for the Supreme Court. As if their behavior surrounding the presidential election wasn't reprehensible enough, they have now exceeded themselves with their recent ruling concerning the Americans with Disabilities Act (ADA). For those who may not have been following the story, the Supremes voted last week to overturn a lower court that had allowed a nurse in Alabama to sue the state—her employer—for demoting her upon learning she had been diagnosed with breast cancer. The Court, it seems, has ruled that people may not sue their employers for disability-related discrimination if that employer happens to be the state. (The rationale for this mean-spirited decision had to do with the cost to taxpayers.) As we might say in this state, it was a wicked bad decision. And one that opens the door to the piece-by-piece dismantling of the ADA, one of the most important pieces of civil rights legislation ever enacted. Of course, I have to wonder what would have happened if the nurse had been a male with testicular cancer. I offer this thought not as knee-jerk feminism, but because of what took place in the state of Maryland, where I used to live. Some years ago, we tried to pass legislation that would force insurance companies to cover the health consequences of DES, a drug to be taken by pregnant women to prevent miscarriages but frequently causing in reproductive tract cancers in their daughters. Only when we demonstrated that male offspring also suffered genital anomalies did the bill pass. Be that as it may, I'm with Senator Patrick Leahy, who has declared the Supreme Court's increasingly Federalist leanings inappropriate and its actions alarming.

Another thing that leaves me gasping for fresh air is a report in the *New York Times* (February 18, 2001) about women whose children have been taken away from them because of prolonged breast-feeding. It seems that in our never-ending wont to consider the female breast a sex object rather than a baby feeder, women who enjoy the natural function of this part of their anatomy for longer than other folks deem appropriate are being positioned as sexual perverts. The latest story, and there are many, involves a 32-year-old Illinois mom whose son still liked nursing at the age of 5. Many of us may consider this a rather long time to breast-feed, but that is beside the point. In a great many cultures, children wean themselves, and they are allowed to nurse until they decide they've had enough. This often takes four or five years to happen. The woman in Illinois was simply following guidelines offered by the LaLeche League, which advises weaning only when the child indicates a readiness to do so. For this heightened maternal instinct, her son was torn from her and temporarily put into foster care by a judge

SANITY FOR ALL IN THE 21ST CENTURY...

who saw "enormous potential for emotional harm" in the prolonged mother-child bond. As Florida attorney Elizabeth Baldwin said in the *Times* article, "We don't have a problem with breasts in other settings, like billboards or string bikinis on the beach. We don't have a problem with children's need to suck, if a five year old sucks his thumb or a pacifier. But put together breast and kids sucking and we think it's a problem of sex." We also think that letting our babies sleep in our beds is a perversion, something that most Asians and Africans find ludicrous. What could be more comforting? they argue. Or more convenient if you are nursing? As one expert put it, "We find our babies irresistible . . . but even as [a mother] feels pleasure in cradling and nursing a baby, a healthy mother remembers that it's for the child . . . to protect and nurture that child." In a society which is known for mother-blaming, sexual objectification, and increasing accounts of childhood sexual abuse, it can hardly be surprising that we view breast-feeding or other intimate mother-child acts as a perversion. To those who jump to such spurious conclusions, and to the Supreme Court, my message is simple: Get a grip!

Finally, and not unrelated to the above issues, I fervently wish that all the young women who claim that they are "not feminists, but . . . " would shake the cobwebs off, open their eyes, and smell the coffee. This semester I teach about 50 of them what women's history, status, and psychology are about. Their class journals abound with accounts of neighborhood domestic violence, striving single mothers, female depression and eating disorders, unacceptable behavior by the boys in the bar, and more. And yet they tell me that they "love guys" and "don't want to be bitchy."

It seems to me that there is a colossal disconnect here somewhere. Until the day that nurses don't get demoted for breast cancer, that women can breast-feed without losing their children, and that young women can stop wearing

Wonder Bras, it seems that women like me will continue to beat our breasts in the name of sanity and compassion. When that fails to be effective, I suppose we can always throw ourselves into a fury of spring cleaning, even if the snow is still on the ground.

WHO CENSORS THE CENSORS?

A few years ago a friend of mine wrote an astonishing and immaculately researched book called *Passiongate: The Conspiracy Theory for the Rest of Us*. It made the case, cogently and without romanticism, that Aristotle Onassis was behind the murders of John F. and Bobby Kennedy, the two men who stood in the way of his claiming Jackie. A well-known publisher expressed serious interest in the work, then hastily and without explanation reneged on its offer to acquire the book. Self-published, it has sold thousands of copies.

Then I learned that a national watchdog group whose sole purpose is to keep track of the most suppressed news stories each year had revealed that a shocking number of important environmental issues never see the light of publication.

Now comes a woman from Putney, Vermont, who has sent me a disturbing book called *Emerging Viruses: AIDS and Ebola—Nature, Accident, or Intentional?* because as she noted in her cover letter, I am "political" and might be able to draw attention to the book and its allegations. The book's author is Leonard G. Horowitz, a Massachusetts dentist with two master's degrees, one of which is from Harvard. Dr. Horowitz is also the author of *Deadly Innocence*, an expose of a Florida dental AIDS tragedy with far-reaching implications that are further developed in his latest work.

Journalists tend to have a knee-jerk reaction to receiving information similar to what the woman in Putney sent me. We want to dismiss it. We are busy, we have our own priorities, we think the source might be a kook. Also, if we are not investigative journalists, the information might hook us, but it just seems overwhelming. Such was the case when I received this book.

Then I read it.

Now I wish Woodward and Bernstein or Joseph Lelyveld of the *New York Times* could be convinced to take it on. Because if Dr. Horowitz's allegations were to prove correct, we would be talking about the most extraordinary holocaust in all of human history: the accidental or intentional infection of humans with the AIDS virus for purposes of experimentation related to biochemical warfare and population reduction.

Numerous authorities, it seems, have suggested that viruses like AIDS and Ebola were laboratory creations transmitted via tainted hepatitis, polio, and smallpox vaccines in the U.S. and Africa. During the Cold War, it is alleged, military contractors (with technical support from such organizations as the World Health Organization) developed numerous viruses designed to ravage the immune system. It is further alleged that they experimented with antidote vaccines for purposes of "national defense" and cancer prevention. Horowitz draws chilling connections between such far-reaching organizations and individuals as the National Cancer Institute, the CIA, Henry Kissinger, and the Rockefellers. While his 600-page book is daunting for the average layperson like myself, I find it credible and alarming. I think it is worthy of mainstream media time.

Just as I think *Passiongate*, critical environmentally related stories, and other suppressed information of national interest are worthy of mainstream media time and attention. Why don't they get it?

That is the real point of this essay. Who is making sure that we don't get those stories? Who and where are the censors who decide what we may know? Who controls the information we receive? Is there really a free press?

Sometimes my friends tease me; they know I am given to conspiracy theories. Laugh if you like, I tell them. But do you really think that if a large corporation with profit as its prime motive owns a major newspaper or TV network you will find out what's really going on within the industry it dominates? Do you actually believe that the CIA or the FBI doesn't have its hands in the information till? After the Tuskegee experiments, Watergate, Ollie North, Gulf War syndrome, and the U.S.-backed debacles of Latin America, do you really still trust government?

We would be wise as a nation, I think, to keep our eyes, ears, and options open. Americans are all too quick to claim "it could never happen here." But things are often not what they seem, even in a flourishing democracy, and a bit of vigilance never hurt anyone. Pollyanna may have her place, but so does healthy skepticism. At this point, that is all Dr. Horowitz is asking of those of us who read his book.

The real question, for now, is: Why is it so difficult for us to find our way to it?

COMMUNICATING CONSERVATION: LESSONS FROM THE DEVELOPING WORLD

Ask anyone abroad what Americans want, and they have a ready answer: They want it all, they say. Big cars, cheap gas, quality health care, superior education, air conditioning, the latest electricity-fed high-tech computers, clean (running) water, and lower taxes. Then they laugh.

If they are from European or other well-developed countries, chances are these folks are paying big time at the petrol station, the liquor store, and the cigarette supplier. In exchange, they have access to well-qualified health providers, universally. Health care is not tied to employment-based schemes, age, or deprivation scales. They also are likely to turn out the lights in empty rooms, to lower the heat at night, and to use public transportation whenever possible. For the most part, these are people who understand that in a time of increasing demand on finite resources, something's got to give, and that reality means a shift in lifestyle.

People from poor developing countries may not have such great health care, but they understand conservation. They've been scraping along in an exhausting and endless attempt at subsistence survival their entire lives. Every scrap of thread they use and reuse has value, and they know instinctively that American opulence and self-indulgence just aren't going to cut it in a world of shrinking firewood, fuel, and potable water.

We have a lot to learn from so-called Third World experience. Take, for example, energy conservation and respect for the environment. Despite the Bush administration's fantasies of endless energy sources (or at least enough to last our lifetimes; then it's every man [sic] for himself), the reality is that we Americans are going to have to learn to curb our appetites, to do with less, to rein in our excesses.

Such behavior change does not come easily. As public health educators know, you can't just tell people what's best for them and expect them to change their values, beliefs, and behaviors. Awareness of a problem is one thing, but how we act and the choices we make are quite another. And sustaining new behavior is yet another uphill battle.

For almost three decades now, international aid agencies like the U.S. Agency for International Development, along with various nongovernmental organizations such as OXFAM and Save the Children, have been investing huge amounts of money, energy, and human resources to effect behavioral change around the world in areas of health, education, nutrition, agricultural practices, child survival, women's status, and the environment. Methodologies that wed science and technology to arts and entertainment have proven to be effective in changing knowledge, attitudes, and practices among individuals, institutions, and communities, and for the most part, in sustaining those changes.

Most of these behavior change models borrow from

commercial marketing to make the "product" they wish to "sell" (i.e., healthy or environmentally friendly behaviors) palatable, to position that product as beneficial, and to promote it in all the right ways and places. Media advocacy, where there are electronic media, creates demand for appropriate public policy, while folk media, soap operas, and music stars "enter-educate." As a result of these communication—based strategies, family planning has been adopted, girls are staying in school longer, food security has replaced handouts, and the environment is being preserved or restored.

In this country, similar strategies have been applied to effect seatbelt use, to reduce forest fires, and to promote healthy hearts. In an extraordinary example, the campaign to stop Americans from smoking went so far as to change social norms in this country forever. Such is the power of a well-orchestrated communication strategy.

So why can't we do it again? It isn't enough to tell Americans that somewhere down the line they may have to give up their SUVs, turn off their computers, or lower their gas consumption. As people in the developing world can attest, it takes a long time and a sustained effort to move beyond knowing. And in the continuum of change that is surely inevitable for us, we would do well to ask our neighbors to the south what lessons they've learned. The quality of our collective future could depend on it.

HAPPY BIRTHDAY, FLORENCE

Ask 10 people what they think of when they hear the name Florence Nightingale, and 9 of them will probably conjure up images of a "lady with a lamp" bringing comfort and fresh bandages to the wounded of the Crimean War. In reality, Nightingale, one of Lytton Strachey's *Eminent Victorians*, was far more than that. In today's terms, she was an expert in organizational development, a human resources manager, a fund-raising specialist, an outstanding administrator, and an advocate. So are many of today's nurses.

Nursing, like teaching, is a horribly underrated profession. Because it is seen as "women's work," an avocation at best, it has always been undervalued. Even in my day (which is to say the 1950s), "nice girls" were dissuaded from taking up nursing. Nurses, like airline stewardesses, were said to be fast, loose, and easy. I suppose this was because nurses knew about bodily functions, and stewardesses traveled alone. You had to be strong of stomach, and will, to do either job, and that just wasn't, well, ladylike.

During World War II, nurses finally got some respect.

But even then, people didn't know the half of what they were doing, and enduring. Take the "angels of Bataan and Corregidor," for example. These 99 army and navy nurses, the only group of American women ever captured and imprisoned by an enemy, spent three years in a Japanese prison camp, ultimately surviving on weeds cooked in cold cream. Before their incarceration they helped build and staff hospitals in the middle of a malaria-infested jungle, pioneered triage nursing, kept a lot of soldiers alive, and helped more of them die. Their strength, humor, competence, and capacity for survival were truly amazing, and they all survived their ordeal largely because of their dedication to the profession of nursing. Only in 1983 did the Veterans Administration finally honor these women. Following the war, Commander Maude Davison was denied the Distinguished Service Medal because General Jonathan Wainright thought "the position of Chief Nurse, although important, is not one of great responsibility."

Then there were the Vietnam nurses. No one knows how many women actually served in that war, but most of them were nurses, and all of them volunteered for duty. When they came home, many suffered psychologically, and few were recognized as true veterans. Lily Jean Adams was one of them. Just 22 years old when she went to 'Nam to work as an intensive care nurse, she remembers what it was like being with someone who was dying. "Sometimes they would say 'Don't leave me!' And I wouldn't. I had an inner sense that [staying with them] was just as important as trying to save the living."

But war nurses aren't the only ones we need to remember during Nurses' Week, which is marked by the May 6 birthday of Florence Nightingale. There are the "ordinary" nurses who fly mercy missions aboard medevac planes (some of whom have lost their lives doing so), the hospital staff nurses whose decisions and "suggestions" save lives every day, the office nurses and school nurses and nurse educators, all of whom quietly make a difference in our lives.

The shortage of nurses is a hot topic recently, but it doesn't take a brain surgeon to diagnose the problems related to recruitment and retention. When docs make big bucks while nurses make beds, when insurance companies dictate while nurses do double shifts, when the real health care providers are viewed as little more than handmaidens, is it any wonder that we can't find enough people with masochistic tendencies to fill the gap?

We may wonder what Florence Nightingale would say if she were alive today. But it's not hard to guess what she would do. Like many of those who followed her, she would no doubt organize, educate, advocate, and lobby—in short, she would clean up the swamp. The very least we can do is to honor her and the sisterhood she spawned. After all, we all need an angel in our lives now and again, even if their Distinguished Service Medals are nowhere to be seen.

THE VIRTUAL RAGE OF A CYBERSPACE AGE

The first time it happened, I had it coming. I'd made the mistake of asking for information by writing to an e-mail address. I simply wanted to know more about an on-line service and thought that a short blurb would be wired my way to which I would reply "Please send more information" or "Thanks, but no thanks." Silly me. What hit my screen the next time I opened my mailbox was a page-upon-page barrage of verbiage the likes of which I'd never seen. Do people actually read this stuff, I wondered? "Help! Get me outta here!" I shot back (or words to that effect), and much to the credit of the source, I was immediately "unsubscribed," as the jargon goes. "It's computer etiquette," a friend said, when I told her how relieved I was. Or was that "computer ethics"?

The next time I was assaulted was more frightening, however, because what hit me was unsolicited, highly political, and a lot messier. It was as though someone had crashed through my front door on the Information Superhighway and littered bodies everywhere. I wasn't sure how to clean it up or, indeed, where the mess had come from. The communication had something to do with race relations at a college in New England, and in addition to the original message asking me to support the hunger strike of a very angry and somewhat paranoid student, there were responses from the college president, rebuttals from a variety of very left of Left organizations, and commentary from various and sundry observers of the situation. How, in God's name, had this mishmash made it into my computer? I looked at the distribution list and immediately figured out that somehow the fact that I write for a publication located in the same city as the college had put me in the firing line. I was sure, therefore, that (a) I would never get out of the loop, and (b) that I would somehow be judged by the entire world to have contributed to the death by starvation of one socially active if somewhat self-righteous student. I was sure my politics would be called into question and expected to start receiving hate mail, threatening phone calls, and all manner of solicitations. Fortunately, none of that actually happened, and although I have no idea why these communications stopped as suddenly as they began, I am deeply grateful and a bit less terrorized by technology. Nonetheless, I remain a skeptic at a time when going on-line is rather urgent. Not only does my professional life depend on it (all advice to writers is that if you're not submitting work electronically, you can forget about competing for editorial attention, and much teaching is conducted via distance learning), but I am only middle-aged and refuse to concede that I am terrified, both technically and spiritually, of what the computer age has wrought.

If you think I'm overreacting, consider this: An article in the *Washington Post* described Orlando, Florida, as "the city where reality is just another design concept," and rightly so. Plans are under way, it seems, to build a virtual Key West, a fake place imitating a real place less than 400 miles away. Such sanitized, themed environments are apparently springing up all over the place. We don't even notice them anymore. Does anyone think it's strange that streams and forests transect hotel lobbies? Are wave pools an anomaly in shopping malls? Are airports that look like Spanish haciendas out of place? As one observer said, "the fake is replacing the real everywhere. Everyone knows the fake is better than the real."

So what has this got to do with computers and the Information Age? Plenty. Because concepts like "idealized reality" and "virtual community" are the epitome of an oxymoron. You simply cannot be real and fake at the same time. For one thing, it's horribly disconcerting and makes for a great deal of confusion when you try to sort out fact from fiction and illusion from real life when it matters most. Virtual anything ends up messing with everything ultimately, from the nuts and bolts of life to attitudes and behavior, values and ethics. And in the end, I believe, all this rapid, high-tech, computer-generated, make-believe-you're-really-there pseudocommunication is going to have horrendous effects on us as a species. I think we humans are mutating so rapidly, both psychologically and socially, that we don't even know it and therefore cannot sensibly assess the effects of the changes taking place in what we think of as our world, much less how we behave toward one another in it.

We have known for a long time what happens to the human soul when it is not nourished. We know it from studies of infant development and from studies of Third World women who still go to the river to wash clothes even when you give them washing machines, so that they can interact. We recognized with alarm the limitations on human development and skill building brought about by technology when we realized that young children could no longer tell time without digital watches and could not do basic math functions without calculators. We see ourselves becoming more aggressive when things take longer than a millisecond to happen. Our powers of concentration are less than they were in the days of reading books, writing letters, and talking to each other. We no longer meet in person to generate ideas. Rather, we voice-mail, e-mail, teleconference. We have forgotten the function of the water cooler.

Does this perspective mean I'm one of those people who would have said to Christopher Columbus, "Don't bother. It's flat," or who railed against sending a man to the moon? Well, I do have my funding priorities. But essentially, I'm not against science and technology. A certain kind of "progress" is inevitable. Computers, like anything else in this modern world, have their place. I love that they've made things like air travel safer (as long as the pilot can override), writing easier, and films more exciting. It's just that I fear things may get out of hand if they take over our lives. As French philosopher Jean Baudrillard has pointed out, "the Age of Absolute Simulation" has meant that there is a dramatic blurring of authenticity, and we must take care. We must never mistake as real those events and places that do not truly exist just because they make us feel happy or powerful. We must not be too impatient to confront each other with real emotion around real issues. Relationships, like ideas, matter. We must not, in short, park our souls at the keyboard.

So while I worry about all the kooks and criminals taking over the 'Net, dread electronic junk mail, and am frightened of who we will be as *Homo sapiens* in the new millennium, I have no desire to throw out the baby with the bathwater. That's why I've hired someone to help me upgrade my equipment and learn to use it to the max, to conquer my overriding technophobia, to get me to http:// and home again.

But I've also told my students, my editors, and my friends that there are limits. I will not read a thesis on the screen, nor will I allow my work to be critiqued by a room full of people whose faces I cannot watch. There will be no indiscriminate sharing of addresses, no random chats, no flirtations, no virtual moments. When I go full speed ahead onto the superhighway, I want to be in the driver's seat. I want to know who I'm riding with. I want to understand where I'm going, how to get there, and how to find my way back. I want to realize the limitations of the space I'm in, and I do not want, ever, to confuse one journey with another.

The prospects seem both daunting and exciting. But so long as my mind and not my mouse is in control, I think I'll be okay. Click.

COURTESIES AND CRUELTIES: POSTCARDS FROM THE EDGE

Nothing would surprise me anymore. I say that every time, and every time, I am surprised. For years, these surprises have overtaken me like shock waves that ripple through your fingers when you touch a wet wire. They leave me stunned and shocked, bereft. Once recovered, I congratulate myself. You're a survivor, I say. You've done it again; come through. It's what I say to my best friend, my brilliant, resourceful, creative friend who has been defeated not once but three times by people who love her, who want her, who move her across country, who call her a "role model," and who don't even phone to say good-bye when she is displaced. We have been consoling each other for years with accolades about our surviving. But each time, there is the wound, the memory of what went before, the surprise.

Like the surprise when my dean called me into his office

on that gray December day and said, "At this point I think the best approach is to announce that you will be leaving and that we wish you well."

Why am I leaving? That's what I want to know. I ask him. "Why am I leaving?" But I know, of course, that it is a rhetorical question. I am leaving because he can't cope with the tension between me and the department chair which has been escalating with my growing popularity among the students. He thinks it's easier this way. He is willing to see me out, in the middle of my contract and four weeks before my class—the most sought after one in the department—is due to start because he doesn't know how else to deal with the demands of a subordinate who cannot tolerate that I will not serve as her handmaiden, that I occasionally say "no" or "why?" or "I don't think so." He is willing to see me out in spite of the fact that I have spent four years of my life helping to build a new program that will soon be its own school, without me. He will see me out even though his gesture is called "irrational" and "irresponsible" by his colleagues and by my students, who write letters of protest.

"Why?" I ask.

"It's not performance related," he says, as if this will make one of us feel better.

It is the same surprise I felt nearly 20 years ago, the first time this sort of thing happened to me. Then, it was shock, a debilitating wave of shock and grief so profound that I took to my bed with it, as I do now. It was the betrayal that was so surprising, so shocking, like ice water thrust at you by someone you have trusted to warm you instead, betrayal after years of commitment and hard work, years of relationships with women who call themselves trustworthy, inclusive, "mentors." When it happened the next time, 10 years later, I recovered more quickly, congratulating myself on surviving again, being less naive. But the sting was pungent, acrid, a familiar fire releasing ashes of despair into thin air.

This time, I was caught off guard because I thought I

was no longer vulnerable—too sophisticated, too mature, too savvy in the ways of the workplace. But the absurdity of the phone call disarmed me.

"I want to pick your brain."

This I have heard often, as if I had been appointed emeritus prematurely.

Then I am grilled about my credibility. It stands to reason: If you want to pick my brain and my bones clean, you must be sure there is nourishment there.

There will be a meeting, she says, but I am not invited. "I need to get up to speed."

So let me get this straight: You want to pick my brain in order to become an instant expert in a complex discipline it has taken me 20 years to master but not invite me to your meeting, and you are going to interrogate me first to see if my information is credible?

I am stunned, like a dozy animal who staggers, stupid and silly, before falling to the ground after being hit by a tranquillizing dart. I am polite, and all the while I am wondering why I am being polite, answering questions as if I were on a job interview. What has happened to my warrior woman? Where have I gone, retreating into places of old pain that are no longer supposed to surprise me? Why do I agree to copy and send copious materials, and why do I cover them with a note that only hints at my distress: "You will understand, I hope, that it is rather like being asked what dress you should wear to the party but not being invited to the party yourself!" (How clever, how witty. Maybe she'll seek my services after all.) Then I apologize if I have sounded aggressive or negative. I apologize!

Some days later, at a meeting, I see this woman who has left me with a dull, throbbing headache and a huge load of displaced rage. I approach her. "I could have brought the documents to you," I say, smiling. (Why am I reduced to such sniveling acquiescence, I wonder, when I am so livid?)

She ignores me, makes it perfectly clear that she has nothing to say to me, not even thank you. I slink away, dismissed.

And then the tears start. Tears that fell 20 years ago, 10 years ago, last December, now. What are these tears about that neither purge nor catalyze me? What are these tears that immobilize me with grief, filling my interior space with such sadness that I feel I will melt into a puddle of pain?

For days, I rant and rail and wave my fists while my best friend, who has also known this pain, tells me that I'm a survivor and says, "I always think that nothing will surprise me. And then I am always surprised." She says "surprised," but she means "hurt." She and I have both been "surprised" in the last four months. These "surprises" are one of the things that binds us.

But still, I do not understand the tears that will not stop coming.

And then one day, I do understand, because I say this to my friend: "How could they not have called you, not one of them who said you had saved their lives? Where is their humanity? What are we without our humanity?"

It is in that moment that I know what I am grieving for. I am grieving for the absence of humanity. Not for the slights of arrogance and rude behavior, not for the competition, not for the hostilities that come from power and position and perception, but for the loss of humanity, the essence of human being that ought to breed courtesy and kindness and civil discourse, even in such mundane domains as offices and meeting halls and telephone lines. It is the absence of humanity that always takes me by surprise, that wounds me and makes me weep, and that I call upon myself, over and over again, to survive. It is the absence of humanity that renders me alone in a crowded room full of people I know. And it is the absence of humanity that so often has chilled my soul as if I were standing in a barren crater where no life can be sustained.

Once, I met a funny psychologist who tried to help people who were always being surprised by the hunger of their souls. She said she refused to carry within her other people's inhumanity. So she carried instead a huge stack of postcards with her, and every time anyone made her angry or sad, she wrote them a note and mailed it at once. On my lighter days, these are some of the postcards I would like to write:

Dear Dean: When you wake up in the morning and look in the mirror to shave, what kind of a man do you see there? It is my fervent hope that for the rest of your life, every day of every week of every year, you will be tormented by this question.

Dear Colleague: You owe me an apology and $10 in copying costs. And by the way, are you always so arrogant, or are you just terminally rude to people you perceive to be lesser human beings than yourself?

Dear Best Friend: You are an inspiration. Never, never lose your humanity! It helps me to survive.

And not to weep over the surprises of the world.

FIFTH AVENUE RAMBLE

On a balmy fall day, the kind when the memory of summer makes you almost believe that December darkness could, by some miracle, be eluded, a woman strolls down Fifth Avenue, wishing for a *deus ex machina* to relieve her angst. She knows, of course, that no divine intervention will intercede in her latest existential crisis, but it's nice for her to imagine that there might be an easy way out of her relentless interior monologue on the issues of Being and Non-being. Her present state of unsettlement, spawned by renewed reflections on some of the cosmic issues of modern life, is a lonely business. It causes her anxiety, near panic sometimes; often, she feels herself trapped by the realities of her era. She wonders, for example, what will become of human beings because of technology and hurry-up time and downsizing and competition, all of which makes us so unkind to one another. She reflects on the fact that there is a fundamental disconnect between people and that no one listens anymore. She knows that her own sense of isolation and alienation is universal, soul destroying, but not many people talk about it; they merely accept it as a condition of adult, urban life. She does not. She wonders where her place is in a world growing ever more insular and self-protective.

Her current crisis has been fueled by rejection. She has been chastised because she asked to be heard on a matter of some importance. Until she became insistent, her superior wouldn't listen, wouldn't take her seriously. Now he has accused her of pushing the limits of his tolerance. Her child-voice says, *I'm sorry! I didn't mean it!* Her adult-voice says, *Chill! I am not the enemy!* She wonders why so many people who purport to respect, even love you feel entitled to rip holes in your heart.

Her mood is exaggerated by the cacophony, the extremes of Fifth Avenue. Limos, winos, Gypsy beggars, women dripping in Gucci, Pucci, and fur; Elizabeth Arden, Bijan, Versace, Tommy Helfiger, Trump, VanClef and Arpel. Who are the ordinary mortals? Does anyone care about the man with a lampshade over his face, squatting in front of Walt Disney & Co.? The guy playing trumpet in front of Coca-Cola with a sign that reads, "Stay a while, give a smile, I'll play for you?" Or the man with drooping eyes, sleeping or dying, whose plea is, "Help me please, homeless with AIDS."

On a cell phone, a man in gray flannel and a striped tie barks, "Goddamn consultants! They think they can . . . . ok, call me! Keep in touch!" Is anybody keeping in touch?

In St. Patrick's Cathedral, people are actually praying. This is reassuring; not everyone is worshiping Wall Street. An exhibit on St. Terese of Liseaux, dead at 24 while still passionately in love with Christ, makes her sad. Who might this child have been, this ingenue; what might she really have taught the world, before it voided empathy, if she had lived?

In the dusk, she ponders conformity and wonders what actually happens when a culture is so homogenized that every hotel, every restaurant, every shop in every city is the same. Gap pap. She thinks about the demise of civil discourse among the self-impressed, about alienation and isolation and the toll it is taking on the collective psyche, about the powerful and the powerless, and how one group continually betrays the other, about fear, apathy, ennui, rage.

In the floral landscape of Rockefeller Center, she tries to get a grip, to return to what is known in Zen as *satori*, the cessation of inner struggle. When it eludes her, she walks toward 57th Street, stopping to drop her last coins in the cup of a beggar woman holding a child with matted hair and huge, searching black eyes. At Bergdorf Goodman, she faces east, braces herself against the growing night wind, and puts one foot in front of the other in search of a destination.

GLUTTONY IN THE GLOBAL VILLAGE:
CAN THIS CONSUMER BE SAVED?

It's really reaching scary proportions, this Age of Globalization and mother-of-all-mergers time. Where does it stop, and, more importantly, where does it leave us little guys, who, after all, want nothing more than systems that work and CEOs who care? Here are just a few examples of the havoc wreaked by the marriage of banks, the merger of communications corporations, the partnerships of airlines, and the like:

My friends arrive at the airport for a simple two-hour journey to be with loved ones at Christmas. Forty-eight hours later, the police are summoned to quell the madding crowds who are still being strung along by a major American airline that can't seem to (a) get its information right, (b) get its aircraft off the ground, and (c) tell the truth to its teary-eyed and exhausted holiday travelers. Closer to home, I can't explain to the telephone company, for the umpteenth time, that it has not—despite what the friendly customer service representative says—corrected my account so that it reflects the appropriate plan we have selected, and therefore we do not, I repeat do not, owe them $768, so could they please restore our service. The furniture giant from whom we bought a sofa and chair 10 months ago has no record of whether we paid so proceeds to sic a collection agency on us, despite our promise to check our own records and pay any outstanding bills there may be. (And the store manager dares to ask, "are we calm yet?" when I remind him, irately, that I am doing him a favor.) The ATM eats my bank card because it is malfunctioning but accuses me of fraud, thus leaving me without so much as a farthing when I am out of town. Sears, having given me erroneous information, is now billing me for a new vacuum cleaner when I should have been given a replacement under the warranty I have carried long enough to purchase at least four new vacuum cleaners. AT&T has yet to send me the refund I am due for closing my account, and now the company financing our car wants to know "when we can expect payment?" even though we have arranged for a direct debit from our bank account on a monthly basis. And all this—it's the God's honest truth— in just one month.

Meanwhile, the nightly news reports that the economy is sound, the stock market is thriving, and we should all be reveling in our prosperity. In the face of collection threats and accusations of criminal neglect, I find it hard to rejoice. It's all well and good for the stockholders, I suppose, but we poor mortals (and workers) draw ever closer to a colossal, collective nervous collapse. While the big boys just keep getting bigger and bigger in the name of globalization and profit margins, we little folk bear the brunt of systems that are totally dysfunctional and out of control, not to mention impersonal and intimidating. Where does it stop? What next? In the name of international competition, are we all to drop down into a bottomless black hole of inefficiency and ineptitude until some dreadful crisis of noticeable proportion finally puts a grinding halt to it?

What if surgeons, pilots, mechanics, and other essential human beings started exhibiting the gross neglect, oversight, and downright stupidity of representatives of large corporations? (Not that many of them haven't already gone the way of faceless demons.) You think Y2K will be chaos! I shudder to think of the Armageddon of one-armed survivors dashing around to avoid aircraft falling out of the sky while being chased by bill collectors brandishing weapons of mass destruction!

Every age, I suppose, thinks that its technology and greed have spawned the ultimate in potential disaster and the imminent demise of the human race. And in each age, no doubt, the doomsday prophets have said, "But this is different! We've never had technology and greed like this before!" But you can't tell me it's not different this time, what with lethal weapons, germ warfare, Internet terrorism, global moguls, and stock market maniacs who will do anything to drive the Dow—and the rest of us with it—over the edge.

I tell you, it's enough to force you into the woods to live off the land, if you could find a patch that isn't polluted and positioned within range of a nuclear plant.

The awful thing is, I think this may just be the beginning of still bigger things to come. Every day, a new and even larger merger is announced, and my mailbox is filled with incentives to buy into the megalomania of corporate America. I don't have time to consider these offers if I wanted to; I'm too busy getting on the blower to correct the day's mistakes and accusations. (This, of course, is futile, since at no time is a human being ever reachable at the other end of the cordless phone—the ultimate symbol of disconnectedness.)

So, like everyone else in the world of little, normal people with faces and names and mortgages and kids to feed and bills to pay, I just go on hoping that the sky will not fall, that good old American ingenuity will come through, that somehow checks and balances will remain operative. What choice do we have, really, in the age of AT&T, CNN, Gap, Dow Jones, Dow Chemical, and the rest, but to remain hopeful that, in the end, it will all sort itself out until the next generation can claim its own disaster fantasies?

Somehow, that attempt at optimism feels futile, rather like the engineer on the *Titanic* who kept claiming that it just couldn't be. He thought technology and progress had made his ship invincible. Little did he know, until he'd slipped beneath the icy, irrevocable waters, that he was the ship's ultimate fool. In the end, you have to pity him, I suppose, but when you're traveling in steerage, it's just a little difficult to feel bad for the poor guy in first class.

A BLAST IN THE DARK

There are pundits everywhere claiming to know why two seemingly intact, if marginal, young boys went on a killing rampage one spring day in the calm suburbs of Colorado. I am not among them; I can't imagine how, or why, children come to the fatal conclusion that violence is exciting and attractive, that immortality rests in destruction and unimaginable grief, that guns equal glory. I'm sure it was all the things analysts have pointed to (with the exception of black trench coats)—the accessibility of weapons, parental blindness, school security, rage and insecurity, fierce TV and video games, and more. But I think there was something beyond this stimulation or that variable; I think the incredible actions of those two boys equal the sum of its parts and that, quite possibly, the fundamental underpinning of all that is symptomatic in their behavior is a sense of alienation across America—an isolation so profound that it literally drives us crazy—that defies age, place, time, or socioeconomic status.

Who among us has not felt it at one time or another? In my own experience, I can recall the utter despair I came to feel living in a city for 30 years in which I felt invisible. My beautifully flowering suburban street was, metaphorically, a vacant lot where loneliness and subliminal fear resided. No one held my key for emergencies, and seldom-seen neighbors barely managed a weak wave in the morning or a tight-lipped hello at night. Self-employed, I spent far too many lonely days waiting for the phone to ring, a symbol of caring and connectedness in a world of e-mail, voice mail, and other high-tech devices aimed at separating us from each other in the name of efficiency. I remember walking the streets like a psychological vagabond in a great wasteland, wishing for a meeting to attend or an assignment that would mean I could spend time with people who were otherwise too busy for civil discourse.

Even more germane to this discussion, I recall as a middle-school child being ignored and taunted by my school mates, who found me different from themselves as a religious minority and as someone with a more mature outlook and behavior because, unbeknownst to them, I was caring for ill parents. I suffered in painful silence, feeling profound sadness. On many days I wept in my solitude. I did not "act out" or turn my loneliness into uncontrolled rage, but perhaps that is precisely what the two boys in Littleton, Colorado, did. Maybe they transcended their own sad isolation by transforming it into a grotesque crime against those who had hurt them.

Once, my British-born husband was stranded in Canada for 10 days because of a problem with his visa. For those 10 days, he went nearly mad with the fear of being shut out and possibly cut off forever from all that he longed for. Such estrangement does amazing things to the human mind, no matter what our age or circumstance.

So, while we cannot claim with any degree of certainty to know what drives children to kill children, or others to commit the atrocities they do, we can, I think, step back from facile explanations that lend themselves to 60-second sound bites. We can take a deeper, broader look at the complexities of modern life that drive some of us to incomprehensible acts. (We can also remove the tools that facilitate such acts.) And we can, I pray, begin to care again about those small acts of kindness and connection that remind us of our humanity and keep us whole.

NIGHT LIGHT

"A cosmic question occurs to some people in far-flung lands: Where has the night gone?"

"Everyone is treated the same way [here] by police officers."

These two quotes, juxtaposed as they are on the same newspaper page on a July day in 1999, strike me, for it seems that they are both about fear, about darkness, about what we are losing sight of.

The first story tells us that in the Middle East, Muslim clerics say it's difficult to find the faint sliver of the new crescent moon because of glare from the ground. In the Arctic, native elders say legends drawn from the winter sky are becoming harder to pass on because village lights obscure heaven's spectral caribou and departed souls. From the Himalayas in India, a retired geologist observes,"The clarity of the sky appears to vary from place to place and seems to have decreased with time in half a century." Some put it less poetically. "It's light trash," they say, meaning that as development spreads, so too do the lights of civilization; "the dark frontier recedes."

In a sad reversal of this observation, so too did the light recede, in the metaphorical sense, when George Turner, a 55-year-old black man in a New England town, was stopped by police on his way home from work one evening. The police, it was reported, felt Turner fit the description of a suspect in an attempted armed robbery. "The only similarity," said an observer, "was the color of his skin." Mr. Turner, it turns out, is 38 years older, 30 pounds heavier, and three inches taller and was dressed differently from the suspect being sought in connection with the robbery attempt.

Clearly, the lights are going out in more ways than one.

Overdevelopment and "racial profiling" are but two of the phenomena we find ourselves grappling with as we look ahead to what Bill Clinton likes to invoke as "the 21st century." Along with road rage, globalization, the superhighway, and various other imprints of the current century, these are two realities we will have to come to grips with, hopefully sooner rather than later.

Blindness, literally or symbolically, is a terrible thing to contemplate. Not to be able to see the night sky in all its splendor represents for many of us a terrible loss, a disconnection from the cosmos, a darkness so complete that we cannot define it. Blindness of attitude, that huge void that renders us incapable of entering into and relishing the family of humankind, is a heinous disease that robs us of the vital light of humanity.

But blindness, in another way, can be enlightening. To be color blind, to see beyond that line which divides us historically by hue, is the gift of perspective, and without it, we are lost in eternal darkness, even though we may not recognize it.

It saddens me to think of the night sky becoming some amorphous, indiscriminate blob of dim light. And it frightens me to think of the racism that lurks in the hearts of so many of us. I want to look up into the face of the constellations, to know that the heavens are bigger than we are, to remember the stories of the sky. And I want to be able to look at the Mr. Turners of the world without prejudice or guilt, and without preconceived notions and mutual suspicion. In short, I want the lights to go off, and I want the lights to go on.

Dare we hope for such balance in the universe?

COURTESY CALLS

I don't know about you, but one of the things that drives me absolutely nuts is being ignored. It doesn't matter who ignores me—my kids, my spouse, colleagues, service people, whoever—I get mildly hysterical at not being responded to, as if I were invisible, a nonentity, not worthy of reply or reaction. Over the years, I've managed to figure out the psychological reasons for my angst on these occasions, which I won't go into in the interest of editorial space as well as my privacy, but these reasons, Freudian or otherwise, aren't what really matters here. What matters is that no one ever calls back, and I'm nearly round the bend as a result!

I first thought that not returning phone calls, or otherwise ignoring people, was an urban phenomenon, something people did under the stress of overcommitment, competition, or self-importance. Now I find it's endemic in rural America as well. In fact, it has become something of a national characteristic, it seems, or worse still, a global epidemic.

When I was still in the formal work sector, I wouldn't think of leaving the office with even one pink message slip on my desk. I returned calls from home if need be and rose in the wee hours of the morning or stayed up late at night if a caller was from another time zone, just to demonstrate that I could be as prompt and courteous as the next one. In those days, as my age group is wont to say, people got back to you within a day or two at the outside. Now, even when their profits are at stake, it seems, it's *manana* or, more likely, never. People have even started ignoring e-mails, something that only months ago, in a state of technological euphoria, we would never have done. Why is this happening?

Have we become so fundamentally discourteous that we think it doesn't matter to keep others waiting, to leave them dangling in suspense about a query or a cry for help? Or is it something worse than discourtesy, an insidious change in how we relate to other people, driven perhaps by the growing distance we all feel from one another because of the pace of our lives and the technology we now consider to be essential? I, for one, worry about things like alienation and isolation and the effects such 21st century realities will have upon us. I long for connection, for the time when responding to someone was considered the day's priority, when the courtesy of a reply went without saying, when RSVP was not only honored but usually unnecessary. Today, it's just ignored.

Nearly every phone call I make now has to be repeated two or three times before I can come to closure. This is not only time-consuming; it also demands an enormous amount of energy and administrative skill. My desk is strewn with sticky notes reminding me that someone or other hasn't yet called back and therefore I will have to follow up. I consider it nirvana when I can actually throw away some of those notes because it means something has actually gotten done and can, in the jargon of journalism, be "put to bed." I have reached a human being, and he or she has responded. It's delicious on the rare occasions when it happens.

So my plea is simply this: May I have the courtesy of a reply? Will you get back to me on that? Can we all "reach out and touch someone?"

Hello . . . is anybody there?

BEYOND MILLENNIAL MIDNIGHT

Nothing happened, really, in the way we thought it might. Airplanes didn't drop out of the sky, no shooting stars arced across the heavens in expository ecstasy, and none of the babies born at the stroke of 12 seemed in the least messianic. Water, fuel, electricity flowed. ATMs did not freeze up, we continued our separate journeys into cyberspace, and life went on quite normally as 99 turned its back and retreated, sullen, into history while 00 loomed large on the horizon like wide-open, unblinking eyes amazed by future hope and possibility.

Neither, to our great relief, did terrorists take over our airports, capital cities, or leading citizens, although this appeared to be a genuine threat at the eleventh hour. No natural disasters of unprecedented proportions occurred to fuel the fantasies of would-be prophets. This, of course, was all good news, but a lot of people seemed disappointed by the lack of arms and Armageddon and by what seemed to them to be a general malaise regarding the magic of bearing witness to a new millennium.

Journalists and commentators all over the world seemed to lament our lack of mindfulness about what had just happened. It was as though without death and disaster, and free from violence and mayhem, our capacity to respond, or at least their capacity to interpret our response, had gone numb, and so we were mildly chastised for not having reacted with more gusto (or, in the case of environmentalists, with more guilt) to the ringing of the clock. Quiet introspection and calm celebration of something as momentous as having witnessed an event that has happened only once before in human history seemed beyond expression in a world that defines its days by perversity and tragic outcomes.

But something did happen; something big and universal and unifying happened to us all. Privately, a great, silent gasp shuddered through us in that moment when we crossed from one century to another—that, in itself, was splendid—but then, when we passed from one millennium to the next, well, that was grand and wonderful and awesome in its hugeness. And we felt, each of us, the stepping over of a threshold from one era to another, as if we were tiny grains of sand shifting upon an unknown virgin shore, and really, it was, in a word, cosmic. That's why so many of us wanted to be with our children and grandchildren, or quietly at home by ourselves, or with close friends. To be sure, there was the Times Square crowd, and the chasers of the international date line, and the kids who threw themselves into partying with a vengeance. Youth and money can make you do some pretty silly things. But for most of us, midnight on January 1, 2000, was a time of reflection, a time to be quiet and self-contained, a time to look back and a time to look ahead, a time to share a moment so special that you daren't squander it on strangers.

That may not have made good copy, but for those of

us privileged to have had it, it was a moment we are not likely to forget. It really was millennial magic.

BEAUTY, HISTORY, CULTURE: WHEREFORE ART THOU?

Having just about concluded a summertime blitz of theaters, museums, concerts, and dance performances, I am once again reminded of the place of art in our lives. Whether "Vermeer and the Delft School" at New York's Metropolitan Museum, chamber music at the Yellow Barn in Putney, "Company for Dinner" at the Hangar Theater in Ithaca, or "Dance, The Spirit of Cambodian" at Jacobs Pillow in the Berkshires, there is no doubt about the role and importance of art in conveying universal beauty, human stories, and national heritage.

I owe my renewed awareness of this reality to the people of Cambodia, who are resurrecting a culture nearly destroyed by the brutal Pol Pot regime, which began its holocaust in the 1970s during the era of the Vietnam conflict. From 1975 to 1979, approximately 2 million people—20 to 25 percent of the country's population—died from starvation, disease, forced labor, or execution at the hands of the Khmer Rouge.

Traditional culture was nearly eradicated, and all performance, religious practice, education, and ritual were prohibited. By some estimates, 90 percent of Cambodia's artists died. And yet, some artists and teachers did survive, and they are working together today to restore to Cambodian culture the centrality of music, dance, theater, puppetry, poetry, and song. Piecing together costumes, building makeshift stages, holding classes and performances, they are managing to bring back to life a cultural legacy based on oral tradition, symbolic dance, and storytelling. Such is the need for beauty, culture, and a remembered history among all peoples.

Some of Cambodia's surviving artists are now taking their stories around the world. To hear them, and to see their performance, is to be moved mightily. During New Haven's annual Festival of Arts and Ideas, there wasn't a dry eye in the auditorium as men and women told their stories. Even the actors wept. Speaking in their native tongue (audience members had scripts in English to follow), the shared narratives were about lost children, disrupted marriages, shattered lives, fear and sorrow almost beyond human comprehension. Dancers portrayed ancient rituals, led by a matriarch who had once graced the floor of the Royal Palace.

At Jacobs Pillow, a collaborative project known as "Dance, The Spirit of Cambodia" reflected the organizers' shared commitment to Cambodian dance and music as a cultural treasure of Cambodia, Asia, and the world. "Our profound respect for these living traditions informs all of our efforts," the program said. "We are proud to share the beauty and complexity of Cambodia's performing arts and to help increase the understanding of the history, beliefs, and values of these extraordinary traditions."

Both the beauty and the complexity of Cambodian dance were amply demonstrated by women who had been sewn into their elaborately shimmering costumes, moving in perfect synchronicity on one foot as their fingers bent nearly backward into gentle arches. And while the stories they danced may not have been fully understandable to an unenlightened audience, the meaning and importance of the dance itself were clear. An entire culture was being reborn, remembered, revered.

During the Holocaust of World War II, even in the atrocity of concentration camps, people created art with pictures, words, music. They did this in part lest we forget. But they also did it because of the unconquerable will of the human spirit to embrace beauty, and to find in its presence solace. Throughout human history, from cave life forward, there has always been image, symbol, sound, movement to capture our life and times. It is in our nature to find beauty even in pain, to seek its comfort, to share its message, to cherish it for its humanity.

That is why all over the world, we line up to enter ticketed exhibits, we smile at comedy and weep at tragedy, we are moved by music and story, exalted by ballet and modern dance. As much as any other nutrient coursing through our arteries, art feeds us. We go hungry without it.

With it, we are nourished and made full. So long as there is one artist alive in the world, she or he will be watched, heard, seen, believed, loved, and remembered. For without that artist, we are not fully realized; we exist as compromised human beings.

I was reminded of this when I watched a Cambodian dancer called Pen Sokhuon, who danced even when she was the emaciated sole survivor of her family in the 1980s. She is the epitome of *kru*, a Khmer word meaning spirit, teacher, healer.

Spirit, Teacher, Healer. The embodiment of Art, unbound, unboundaried, timeless. Art not only for art's sake, and for the sake of all our souls.

TILL DEATH DO US PART

"The more things change, the more they stay the same" has never seemed more true.

A few nights ago, I finally caught up with *The Gladiator*. The next night, while driving home in the hot dusk of early summer, I happened upon portions of NPR's "The Execution Tapes." And there it was: In the space of 24 hours, 2000 years of human history had disappeared before me. Or perhaps it was simply reduced to one painful reality. We are an extraordinarily violent species.

Its merits notwithstanding, *The Gladiator* is a blood-and-guts flick. Viewers loved it. Just as the Romans who attended human massacres—the equivalent, I suppose, of modern-day movies—had loved watching men tear each other from limb to limb.

They, of course, were not all that different from 18th-century French peasants who reveled as the guillotine fell, or from white southerners who ate popcorn and cheered as they watched black men swing when public lynchings flourished in the 1930s.

Why should I have assumed that we are any different?

The NPR program I heard, and which was discussed the

next morning on the Diane Rehm Show, was inspired by the debate over whether Timothy McVeigh should be publicly executed by way of TV. The call-in discourse I heard amazed and sickened me.

First there was Phil Donahue making a strident case for public execution as a First Amendment right and a journalist's due. Arguing that we get to watch all kinds of other things on TV (like the assassination of JFK) and that reporters have a right to access, Donahue went off on a diatribe of shrill non-sequiturs that sounded like a child begging for more candy. One caller suggested that it would be educational to view executions, citing the Learning Channel as a model. Apparently, this guy thinks a Death Channel would be something worthwhile. Who knows, it might even have Thursday night reruns of "This Is Your Death!" There is an industry known as enter-educate, in which entertainment is used to promote socially beneficial behavior. Maybe we could foster something along the lines of exe-educate. Its tag line might go something like this: This is your brain. This is your brain after it has been fried.

In fairness, there were some callers who were deeply distressed at the thought of public executions. Someone said the aired tape of a 1954 execution sounded like Nazis calmly recording the events in a gas chamber. Others mentioned human dignity, although the word *morality* was conspicuously absent from the reactions. But for the most part, callers favored the right to see someone put to death, and it is this vote for state-supported violence that leaves me with the terrible belief that something has gone horribly wrong.

Some years ago, in another commentary, I made the case that we were mutating as a species in ways we are not able to comprehend. This, I argued, was due at least in part to technology that depersonalized our lives to such an extent that we no longer knew how to exercise civil discourse or behavior. I now wonder if we have changed at all. Perhaps desensitizing death has always been part of our collective psyche. Even worse, maybe we've always found it awesomely entertaining.

In what may seem a bizarre juxtaposition, I recall the Anita Hill—Clarence Thomas hearings. Here is what they had in common with the current debate: Both events are a prime example of what Freud called "reaction formation." As Psych 101 students know, the term refers to the sublimation and denial of our baser instincts. In short, we compulsively clean ashtrays because we secretly wish to grovel in dirt. Or as Senator Orrin Hatch implied during the Hill—Thomas hearings, these are disturbing events but we must talk about (or see) them.

On its program, WNYC, an NPR affiliate, asked callers why they chose to listen and what they felt. Here is my answer. First, I felt betrayed by NPR because it had gone the way of tabloid journalism. Then I felt afraid; the mutations I have long feared were rearing their ugly heads. I was sad. I was outraged. I was incredulous. But I listened. Why? Because inside the heart of all of us lurks a voyeur. Just as we secretly harbor homophobic or sexist or racist tendencies about which we may be unaware until put to the test, I think we are all unable to turn away from the scene of the accident. Gladiators grab us. Guillotines fascinate us. Lynchings are horribly seductive.

And that is exactly why we must follow the moral imperative by disallowing public execution. Not because it is unlikely to be a deterrent. Not because it is less likely to educate (whom, and about what?). Not because the public has no right to know what has happened at state expense. But because if we are to call ourselves human beings endowed with dignity and a moral sense, we must reject violence in all its forms. We must bring death back into the realm of the private. And above all, we must be able to look our children in the eyes and say to them, with the fullest conviction, it is life—not death—that matters.

A BREATH OF
FRESH AIR

Day 15 and I'm exhausted. I've been to a circus, a playhouse, a swimming hole, the Vermont Country Store, the Dari Joy, the playground, two museums, a boating lake, the Yankee Candle Company, plus every neighbor and friend I can think of. Having two energetic children with the attention span of normal 8-year-olds is no easy thing. Luckily, I'd forgotten that fact when we volunteered to serve as a host family for the Fresh Air Fund.

When I first thought about becoming a Fresh Air mom, my granny fantasies ran rampant. I imagined baking cookies, cutting peanut butter and jelly sandwiches into shapes with cookie cutters, supervising art projects, and reading copious bedtime stories. I told my husband, "You can write a check, or you can change a life." Two days into the visit of my little girls, I was buying cookies, slapping bologna between two pieces of white bread, providing crayons and blank white paper, and managing two pages a night of *Julie of the Wolves*. Having now bid the girls farewell, both my husband and I are catatonic, a checkbook in one hand and a stiff scotch in the other, but we wouldn't have missed the opportunity to actually make a difference in these kids' lives. Or ours. I loved those nighttime hugs, the sound of "Mom!" when I was too long out of sight, the wide-eyed amazement of a child's first encounter with farm animals, the grins and laughter, and "flowers are beautiful" notes I found lying around. While I won't miss the clutter and chaos, it isn't the same in the morning without their little faces peeking around the corner of our bedroom to whisper, "We're up!"

At first they were so shy I didn't know how I would draw them out. At the bus pickup, they barely whispered "Yes" or "No" when I asked a question, and eye contact was nil. That lasted all of an hour. By the time we'd eaten our first dinner together (over which a long and silent grace was offered by my new guests), the sound of children's chatter filled the house. In a matter of minutes, it seemed, shoes, clothes, crayons, and assorted other kid signs were strewn about. It was clear that for the next two weeks clutter would reign.

My girls couldn't have been more different from each other. One was self-confident verging on bossy; the other needed lots of reassurance and TLC. The petite one ate like there was no tomorrow, while the sturdier of the two nibbled and picked at her food. One led, the other followed, and they got along like best pals, even though they had never met before.

Everything amazed them—cows, horses, feeding our ducks, chasing butterflies, finding a garter snake under the deck—but nothing more so than the thought that you didn't have to lock your car or house against "bad people with guns." Once when I yelled for them to get out of the tub to see a rainbow, they thought the house was on fire. Urban life takes its toll. But if you want to see youthful joy and curiosity, take a kid swimming, or to the Montshire Museum or to see glass being blown. Ask them to keep a daily journal, then read it with them. Have them make a collage. Eat outdoors.

Not that my kids were angels. They pushed the edge of

the envelope plenty. But a simple "no" or a smiling "because I said so" seemed sufficient and was usually met with a cheerful "okay" and a big smile that suggested, "just thought I'd try that one on."

For the girls, two weeks "with my camp people" meant a break from concreted city life, pollution, urban fear, congestion, and cramped quarters. For me, those two weeks were a constant quest to organize, supervise, and improvise. But when it was over and they'd gone home happily while I regained my equilibrium, I knew we both felt better for the experience.

It just goes to show you what a simple breath of fresh air can do.

WAITING FOR HEAVEN

We are in a bed 'n' breakfast on the Canadian side of the Thousand Islands. It's a lovely house, circa 1890, overlooking the water. Colorful flower beds surround an expansive porch dotted with comfortable rocking chairs, and tea is served upon request. It's a place frequented by "the newly wed and the nearly dead," and our breakfast companions are a set of each.

The newlyweds are shy and quiet, glancing at each other adoringly at regular intervals. The retired couple, from Florida, chat incessantly. They've just moved to a gated, over-50 community and are waxing not so eloquently over its virtues.

"It's heaven's waiting room," says the man, smiling broadly. "That's what we call it."

"Such nice people," his wife chimes in. "We all joke about our operations and illnesses. Everyone takes care of one another."

My husband and I glance across the table at each other and try to refrain from rolling our eyes. We can think of nothing more nullifying than staring at the same golf course every day while sharing stories of hernias and heart attacks with our neighbors, no matter how delightful they are.

ELAYNE CLIFT

We have friends who swear by Elderhostel vacations, and I know that they are filled with erudite seniors studying art, history, and culture. Still, we resist the notion of traveling in a bus full of soon-to-be geriatrics basking in the safety of rapid evacuation in the event of an emergency.

My reflections on this topic are not about ageism. They are about integration. I worry about our increasingly segregated society and ways of living—the boundaries that exist between rich and poor, black and white, Hispanic and Asian, old and young. What is the price we pay when the diversity of community life is gone?

When I was growing up, I lived on a street inhabited by Jews, Irish Catholics, Southern Baptists, young families starting out, middle-aged working folks, and some special elderly people who taught us the wisdom and humor of age. (Sadly, the only blacks we knew were the ones who worked for people like us.) My aunt and uncle, immigrants from the Ukraine, owned an appliance store in Philadelphia in a Polish neighborhood where kids talked in mixed idioms and parents traded ethnic recipes and remedies. We still laugh about some of the things we said and did in those days when the joy of life resided in something so simple as a Polish pastry.

Twentieth-century writer and theorist Charlotte Perkins Gilman, a feminist socialist at heart (although she would have rejected both terms), envisioned communities not unlike Jane Addams Hull House, where everyone lived together, shared responsibility, and learned from each other. The old helped the young, and vice versa, the rich helped the poor (in real rather than *noblesse oblige* terms), the healthy tended the sick, and so on.

I'm not Pollyanna. For one thing, I know Gilman was homophobic and could be anti-Semitic. Clearly, racism ran rampant as new waves of immigrants became part of the so-called melting pot. Old people can be burdensome, just as too many kids underfoot can be annoying. Still there is something gone from those days of stoop sitting and block parties and communal mothering that we like to remember now. We are losing something vital, I fear, in our bifurcated, dichotomized, segregated lives. The highway to heaven is looking more and more like a series of ghettos in which you check your diversity at the door. Gated communities? Elder hostels? No children? Silent quotas? No thanks! Give me a neighborhood of noisy kids, spicy scents, different dress, and cacophonous culture any day. It may not be familiar or entirely comfortable, but at least on my way out, I'll know I've actually been somewhere.

HOHUM HOMOGENEITY

Back in the 1960s, when I first traveled to Europe, every new place was an adventure. Barely into my 20s, I didn't know an Alp from a Pyrenees, a pound from a pence. But, oh, the fun in figuring out what a guinea or "two-and-six" was worth in American dollars. Then there was the shock of what showed up on your plate when you pointed to something on the menu. I remember selecting a veal dish and being presented with a succulent brain, which I have loved ever since if prepared by a French chef. And the thrill of bargain hunting at Marks & Spencer or a small jewelry boutique on the Ponte Vecchio or a book stall on the Left Bank!

Of course, all that was pre-Gap pap, globalization, and transnational mega-markets. Now Bucharest might as well be Boston. On a business trip to Romania's capital city only a few years after "Ceausescu time," I was shocked to see a Benetton's, the first of the Western trendsetters to have infiltrated Romania's emerging capitalism. Boycotting its brilliant colors and skinny mannequins, I made straight for Roma, the communist-era department store for foreigners. There the merchandise is scarce, drab, and tacky, and bored, buxom women with frumpy dyed black hair huddle hostilely in a corner, glaring at you if you purchase something they cannot afford. Then I headed for the local commie restaurant draped in red velvet with husky waiters who were probably once Securitate police. Now that's the Romania I wanted to experience, not the pizza-parlored, boutiqued, cosmetic shop lined-boulevards of Bucharest's burgeoning and Western-inspired bourgeoisie!

The homogeneity of Europe, and the world, seems inevitable. But how sad, especially for those whose first foray to "the old country" comes at a time when originality seems lost to so many cultures. What thrill is there in a Grand Tour when Nicky Hilton, Eddie Bauer, and Tony Roma dominate the landscape from Paris to Prague? What fun is a euro when you've been spoiled by a franc, a mark, or thousands of lira? How do you find your way around a new city when increasingly the landmarks are global golden arches?

Of course, the same dull, predictable landscape dots our cities, too. Gone are the days when the Boston shopping scene meant foraging through the three-dollar tables in Filene's basement, or Chicago was for making a beeline to Marshall Fields and the Magic Mile. How many people even know about Durgin Park or Ed Debevic's anymore? Is staying at Palmer House or The Drake any more fun than, say, crashing at an airplane hangar Hyatt or a Holiday Inn?

Not long ago I returned to the neighborhood where I lived for 13 years while raising my kids. It used to be fun. On winter days you could walk up the hill to the local shopping center for hot chocolate and cookies, and in the summer, the trip was rewarded with jimmy-topped ice cream cones. The hardware store, the Hallmark shop, and the drugstore were all full of fabulous bits and pieces to explore. Everyone at the cleaners, the bank, and the barbershop knew you. Now the old Grand Union has been replaced by a monument to decadence called Sutton Place Gourmet—all brass, glass, chocolates, and wine. The children's store that sold Carter's and Health-Tex has given way to kitsch for kids, and Whirligigs and Whimsies makes FAO Schwartz seem like a five-and-dime. Vanities and Body Line cater to young matrons who come by regularly to sweat out suburban life, literally. Persnickety and Down offer the latest in futons and feathers, and Chez Nous caters nouvelle cuisine.

What I want to know is where do you go when you want white underwear, a three-way lightbulb, or a belated birthday card? What happens when you realize you're out of milk? And most important, who do you drink hot chocolate with when the snow starts falling?

The global economy may have its merits, and world trade might mean world class to some folks. Me . . . I'd give my last crown for a cuppa in a quiet lane somewhere. Anywhere at all so long as the only MacDonald was a farmer and the only burgher a king.

MARGINAL MATTERS

When I was in high school, I had a history teacher who claimed I asked too many questions. It struck me then, as it does now, as an absurd allegation. Surely, if I was a student and he was a teacher, he would want me to ask questions! Then one day, when he couldn't answer one of my questions, he said, in front of my peers, "The trouble with you is, you're a rebel!" I delighted in the label. To me, it meant I stood up to authority and stood for social justice. I've been rebelling one way or another ever since, and I consider myself to be in excellent company.

I remembered that formative experience not long ago when a local teacher, gifted and dedicated from all accounts, was unilaterally fired for showing his students a controversial film in class. The gestures of support that enveloped this particular teacher made me think of all the people who are punished in the workplace for innovation, for truth telling, for risk taking, for creativity, and of just how important such individuals are for all of us.

History is rich with the stories of writers, artists, scientists, voyagers, and others whose theories, life's work, or actions were ridiculed. Many of these stories are tragic. For example, the Victorian physician who first understood that women were dying of preventable infections from contaminated hospital births was driven mad by disbelieving colleagues for advocating simple hand washing as an antiseptic method. Less sad but no less important are the tales of artists (like many of the Impressionists) whose work was valued only posthumously. Experimental writers like Virginia Woolf, innovative social philosophers like Charlotte Perkins Gilman, and activists like Margaret Sanger suffered untold criticism and abuse, and the National Women's Hall of Fame in Seneca, New York, abounds with stories of other women whose pioneering work was dismissed, plagiarized, trivialized, and condemned by others.

I once wrote a story about whistle-blowers—people who told the truth in the workplace, perhaps because conditions were unsafe, or the product was faulty, or sexual harassment ran rampant. Every one of the two dozen people I interviewed was a true hero in my book, although each was fired and labeled depressed, dysfunctional, insubordinate, unfit, disloyal. Like Karen Silkwood, or the women who blew the whistle on Love Canal, or the woman who lived in a tree for months to save a forest from being felled, each of the people I interviewed had taken a risk in the interest of the greater good.

Each of these whistle-blowers, like the writers, artists, scientists, and others history now immortalizes—and like the local teacher who first made me think about this topic—suffered deep humiliation. Each, at least for a time, was marginalized by his or her community. Each had demons to fight, whether public or private. Some recovered and moved on; many did not.

It is important, in my view, that we understand what motivates good people who are willing to take risks in order to enlighten others, improve our quality of life, remedy ills, strengthen resolve, challenge complacency. Such brave souls deserve our respect, not our ridicule. Would that we all had the courage to foster creative thinking for the collective good.

My curiosity all those years ago didn't deserve to be publicly denigrated. People who "think outside the box" don't deserve it either. The teacher who thought he could engage his students by deconstructing a controversial film had the best of intentions, and from all accounts, would probably have succeeded in appropriately challenging his students, given the chance. Those brave souls who told the truth about their workplace or their environment should have been rewarded, not chastised to the extent that many of them could not find subsequent work, reminiscent of the McCarthy era.

The fact is that without those risk takers who are so often sidelined, there would be no forward momentum. One of history's lessons is that the marginal benefit the many, over the long term. Without their visionary thinking, their courageous acts of rebellion, their new ways of looking in the mirror and telling us what they see in its shiny reflection about our own times, there would be no progress.

I'm not as brave as many of the people I'm thinking about as I write this essay. But I'm glad I still "ask too many questions" and like to be in the company of "rebels." When it comes to mainstream or marginal, I know exactly where I'm most comfortable, and that, it seems to me, is what matters in the end for each of us.

PHARMACY FOR DUMMIES

I used to be involved in health education in developing countries, where often the 10 or 20 percent literacy rate meant that only a few (usually men) could read and write. This presented serious challenges in crafting health messages that people (mostly women) could understand. It was critical that visual instructions be clear, because mistakes in mixing or administering something like oral rehydration solution or various medicines could be lethal.

Now it seems the FDA has to take a look at lessons learned abroad.

Following alarming revelations about medication errors in Canada recently, it has now come to light that an estimated 1.3 million Americans are injured each year from similar errors. And according to a report in the *Brattleboro Reformer* (January 1, 2002), "Nobody knows how many injuries are caused by drug mix-ups, although some studies suggest name confusion is to blame for 30 percent."

This is serious stuff. Not only does it suggest that our own literacy rates may leave something to be desired, but imagine what would happen if you took medicine to cure a fungus (Lamisil) and ended up with epileptic seizures from

Lamictal. Or supposing you were given infertility treatment (Serophene) when you didn't need it, instead of Sarafem when you did. That's enough to drive anyone to Prozac, which is really Sarafem. Then there's Zyprexa and Zyrtec. One is for schizophrenia, the other an antihistamine. So you could have a simple sniffle and end up believing it was planted in your nose by a Martian. (Or you could think the Martian who is after you has gone and dried up all your sinuses, as if you didn't have enough worries.)

It's not all the fault of the pharmacist who fills your prescription, or the nurse who administers your meds in the hospital, or even the doctor who never learned to write in legible cursive. The patient is also being told to be vigilant. According to the Institute for Safe Medication Practices, consumers must take responsibility for checking their prescription drugs carefully and for questioning pharmacists, nurses, and doctors. I'm not sure how, exactly, you do this when you are experiencing such prediagnostic or preoperative anxiety that you are riddled with Valium (we hope), or when you are in a groggy post-procedure state. I can hardly imagine questioning your doctor's authority on a routine visit with any satisfaction.

"So, uh, would you mind telling me what you just wrote on that prescription pad?"

"What dose did you say I should have?"

"Can I just check where that zero is?"

"Is that 25 mg. Or 2.5?"

"Aren't my pills white?"

I've been labeled "noncompliant" for far less than that in my long history as an activist consumer.

Not to worry, though. The FDA has learned a great deal from countries as diverse as Nepal and Nigeria, and it is now taking no chances. It will soon ask pharmaceutical manufacturers to use color-coding, capital letters, and "shelf-shouters," an attention-grabbing card designed to stop pharmacists from taking the wrong bottle from the shelf.

Still, I plan to take an advocate with me whenever I have to go near a medical facility from now on. I want to know what I'm taking, why, and how much. If my providers don't like it, tough. They can take an aspirin—or was that an Aderal?—and call me in the morning. If that doesn't work, I'll take a powder. I'd rather do that any day than take a pill meant for someone else whose problem may be a whole lot worse than mine.

WHERE IS THE P IN PUBLIC RADIO?

I am among those people increasingly troubled by recent trends in public radio, nationally and locally. Not long ago, you might have noticed, after a marketing guru had looked at the bottom line and advised public radio stations that more talk would mean more bucks, the content of NPR, NHPR, and other stations changed dramatically. So, it seems, did the demeanor and raison d'etre of station managers.

I go back a long way with public radio. I lived in Washington, DC, when it first hit the airwaves, and I have had the privilege of appearing on "All Things Considered" back in the days when Susan Stamberg was making a name for herself. I knew the executive producer of ATC when she was an aspiring intern at NPR. Some of its finest reporters in the early days were my colleagues and friends.

So I can speak with some authority when I say that in the early days, NPRers were inspired, innovative, risk-taking, and responsive folks. So were the liberals who listened to them with slavish devotion to the alternative they provided to commercial radio. For many of us, they were the voice of intelligence and sanity in times of turmoil and national tension. They were also a wonderful source of various cultural pleasures, ranging from interviews and book readings to music of all sorts, including jazz, folk, and the classics.

In the old days, accessing public radio with ideas, commentary, questions, or program ideas was fairly egalitarian. You didn't need to know somebody; a good idea or piece would receive its due. Not so today, where queries and professional submissions fall down a bottomless rabbit hole, submission guidelines change daily, and no one seems to feel it incumbent upon them to offer the courtesy of a reply. This is particularly irritating in view of the fact that every time you turn around, there is yet another fund raising pitch in the mailbox or another disruptive telephone solicitation.

According to its mission statement, NPR aims to "challenge and invigorate by a deeper understanding and appreciation of events, ideas and cultures." Other public radio stations promise "stimulating programming" and "rich diversity." They also claim to "want to hear from you." Lately, I have my doubts.

Not that I am trying to throw out the baby with the bathwater here. Public radio is still, "all things considered," a national treasure. So far, it does, for the most part, offer quality programming. Although many of its critics see it tilting far too close to commercial stations than it once did, it is still the only alternative we've got. But concerns about its future deserve serious consideration and have many listeners appropriately worried. For example, if public radio forfeits its original vision and purpose, if it goes the way of six-figure consultants who advocate market-share methods in lieu of cutting-edge journalism and analysis, what will make it any different from other stations? Where will we find intelligent discourse when we want it, or the soothing sounds of classical music when we need it? Surely we can get all the talking heads we need on TV and all the verbiage we can take in print. But where, oh where, shall we find that balanced mix of intelligent radio journalism and inviting entertainment that made public radio so rich in its origins, so unique in its perspective, so right in its diverse offerings?

And if it forfeits its original values, how will we make our own voices heard, whether commenting on or creating program content? How shall we ordinary folk participate in public discourse? If public radio relinquishes its commitment to inclusivity—which means that it reaches beyond its established stable of writers and commentators to welcome the voices of others—how will we be sure that the public airwaves are truly serving, and including, the public? If station managers and producers fail to respond to that public, what is the message in that silence?

The *P* in public radio is about a philosophy and a process. It is about public relations in the best sense of that term. It is about progressive reporting and populist views. It is about the plethora of programming that serves its entire listening audience.

In short, it is about people, not profit. I hope its gurus will keep that in mind next time they look at the balance sheets.

SABBATICAL

The semester is over, the onerous editing and grading of papers is finished, notebooks are filed away, there is time to reflect once more.

Having a semester off, as I do now, is a good thing. Sometimes I get tired of the sound of my own voice, and I think, "Don't you know this yet?" forgetting that to my students, the information is new. I get crabby about the absolute exploitation of adjunct faculty, without whom most colleges would simply have to shut down. I bemoan the fact that high schools just don't teach kids how to write or think anymore.

But then I remember why I do it.

I think of all the times students have said to me, "This course changed my life." (Women's Studies will do that to the uninitiated.) "Thank you so much for making me think about new ideas." "I loved that book!" Or my two all-time favorites: "I'll never not vote again!" And "I'm really gonna help my mom when I go home. I never realized what she went through to raise three kids on her own." Music to my ears.

I remember the adult students I've worked with in graduate or adult degree programs. Students like Hannah, an exquisite woman in her 30s who was widowed several years ago. She lives in Iceland with her three daughters. She writes for a newspaper, walks in the woods a lot, struggles to stay connected to the larger world, and works hard to write solid papers in English. Her goal is to be a literary writer, and I have no doubt she will make it. Her profound sensitivity and gentle searching mean that she is one with the world, even though in her moments of struggle she doubts me when I tell her so.

Jack is an ex-felon and recovering alcoholic. He could have folded years ago, but he didn't. Instead, he started a prison program for recovering substance abusers, built it into a business that now contracts with the state of Texas, and wrote a manual on the subject based on the 12 step programs. Jack still struggles to write well, but he has a keen mind. Sharing ideas with him is pure pleasure, and there is not a gentler soul in the world. Jack and I worked together on a study of spirituality. When his study ended, he presented me with a brass statue of a little boy reading a book. "Thank you for opening up the child in me," he wrote on the card. Every time I look at that little statue on my desk, I think about Jack, who dropped out of school to care for his very ill wife. I hope he will continue toward his degree.

T.J. is someone who taught me about courage and humor and self-acceptance. A transgendered male, he is one of the bravest people I know. Would that we could all find our way to wholeness as he has and feel as comfortable about who we are. A forester, T.J. speaks often and honestly on college campuses and elsewhere about his experience, and I have never seen anything but the utmost respect when he tells his story.

Ramin is an Iranian physician. He studied with me while earning his master's degree in public health and now works in a New Haven hospital. Ramin is a human rights activist who has worked voluntarily overseas to bring relief to victims of war and political upheaval. He and his significant other work tirelessly on behalf of the politically and economically oppressed, and yet he always has time for a visit, a laugh, a meal.

Pamela is an undergraduate who wants to be a psychologist. Her life story reads like something from a grade B novel, complete with sexual abuse, psychiatric incarceration, foster care, and more. She is the first person in her family to attend college, having been told she would never qualify. Pam is a true diamond in the rough. She can be crude and unsophisticated even as she talks about loving opera, theater, and fine music. Her communication skills need some serious work. But the twinkle in her eye belies her struggle for sheer survival, and if she can make it through graduate school, she will be one fine, empathetic therapist.

These students, and others like them, enrich me immeasurably. On a bad day, they help me remember why I allow myself to be used by a system and a society that so devalues the role of teacher that we earn no more than minimum wage in some settings. On a good day, they remind me that I have chosen a noble path and am proud to journey there with such fine human beings.

So while I will enjoy my sabbatical, and am happy to hang up my grade book for a time, I'm sure that when my next gig comes around, I'll be only too eager to get back in the classroom. It may not be a glamorous or remunerative workplace, but that little brass boy on my desk always brings me back to why I am there. Egotistical as it may sound, I just can't wait for the next time someone tells me I made a real difference in their life. Or, for that matter, their mother's.

ON VALENTINES DAY, A LITTLE GIVE-AND-TAKE

The world is obviously made up of lots of people, and it's all too easy to polarize them as either good or bad, smart or stupid, attractive or ugly, funny or dull, kind or cruel. Such categorization is, of course, unfair and simplistic. But when it comes to generosity, there are clearly two types of folks: givers and takers.

The significant other who loves you desperately but can't make a commitment is a taker. The friend who calls routinely when feeling needy but who can't seem to stay in touch when things are going swimmingly is a taker. Many corporate executives are takers. (Just ask a few former Enron employees, who didn't know the big boys were selling.) People who always take a penny from the penny pot but never put one back are takers. Children are takers—it's their job.

Mothers are givers. (It's their job, too.) Volunteers are givers. Friends who are always there for takers are givers.

Good life partners are givers. And most of the time, givers don't even think about it; they just instinctively give up their seat on the bus.

We've all run into our share of takers—people who drain us and then disappear as if they'd been vaporized. I've been "dissed" by a woman who lived in my house for a month when she needed to leave hers, by a boss who thought I was the golden girl while he needed me but who conveniently forgot about that when one of his cronies wanted my job, and by a former boyfriend so big into taking that he didn't even notice when I was gone.

I've also been gifted with giving by people I couldn't live without: my husband and kids, colleagues who really care about me, my beloved circle of Crones who make me laugh, neighbors bearing food and friendship, women who close ranks when I am the needy one, students grateful for their journey with me, children I'm close to whose very presence is a blessing. One of the most wonderful givers I've ever known was my mother. Just being with her could turn you instantly into a taker because of her enormously generous spirit. Being with that kind of giver fills you up as if your soul got mixed up with your stomach. You are never empty. And best of all, you learn the joy of giving yourself.

So this little essay is my Valentine's Day card to the world's givers. What better time to remember all those selfless souls, unsung heros and heroines, good Samaritans, moms and dads, and chums near and far who make life worth living. In these times of stress and self-absorption, of distrust and fear, of international aggression and angst, I want to stop for a minute to remember good, giving people and to say thank you to them, just for being there. They are truly life's treasures.

I have only one question to pose to them as I contemplate their gifts to the rest of us: At the risk of sounding like a taker, will you be mine?

THE FUTURE IS NOW

I have seen the future, and it is now. It is terrifying, and it is real. In the space of just 24 hours, I have had occasion to contemplate the threat of nuclear disaster, bioterrorism, and fascism. Not a pretty picture.

If I was worried before about the possibility of an accident or terrorist attack at the Vermont Yankee Nuclear Power Corporation, I am positively catatonic after attending the town meeting in Brattleboro convened by Representative Bernie Sanders. Sanders did the community a real service by organizing a forum for concerned residents to ask questions and express their collective anxiety to a group of assembled spokespersons. The panel of respondents offered far less. Remarks and responses from Vermont Yankee, the local Federal Emergency Management Agency, and the regional office of the Nuclear Regulatory Commission were less than confidence-inspiring, and like many others, I took particular umbrage at patronizing and ill-informed replies to serious, research-based questions. It is simply unacceptable, in addressing questions about evacuation plans, to say "we need to review our plans more carefully" or "more often" and to render assurances that concerns are being "taken to heart."

It is widely known that Vermont Yankee was one of only three nuclear facilities in the country to be given a yellow safety rating for failing a mock terrorist attack recently. (That's only one step away from the dreaded red alert.) How dare officials say that the security system is "robust" and that it is only our own fear we must resist! What kind of insanity is it to say that we must rely on the goodwill of our neighbors to ensure that nothing goes wrong? What are we to think when a physician reveals that Brattleboro Hospital could never cope with nuclear tragedy, while seven stories of spent fuel rise above an elementary school?

The morning after the town meeting, I listened to the Diane Rehm Show on NPR. It offered a spirited discussion about the very real possibility of smallpox being unleashed, and what the U.S. health care infrastructure might be able to do about it. Again, less than reassuring.

Then my husband and I confessed to each other that we both wondered if the latest government "high alert" for possible new terrorist activity was, in fact, true. With the recent cutbacks in civil liberties espoused by Mr. Ashcroft and his cronies ("Trust us—Big Brother would never abuse these powers!"), wasn't it entirely possible that the administration was scripting its own power grab? I even found myself wondering whether the CIA is the culprit in the apparent abduction of a highly respected scientist in Memphis recently. Maybe we, not Al Qaida, want to pick his brain. Who knows?

Such suspicion is the first sign of a weakening democracy, where no one trusts anything the government says. Before long, it isn't just government rhetoric we don't trust. It is our neighbors, our friends, our sisters, our husbands, our sons (and our police, especially when they shoot people in churches, no questions asked). If you think I'm exaggerating, ask anyone who survived Ceausescu time in Romania (where one in four were members of the Securitate secret police) or the Cultural Revolution in China.

It could reasonably be argued, I suppose, that my

fantasies of fascism are somewhat premature. But no one can deny that the smallpox threat is real, or that seven stories of toxic waste looming nearby are something to worry about, terrorists or not. At no other time in human history, it seems to me, have the earth's inhabitants been subjected to such a real possibility of annihilation, one way or another. While I don't want to be the voice of doom, I do think Armageddon feels less and less like a Bible story and more and more like an unimaginably imaginable scenario—one over which we have precious little control.

I'm not exactly sure what we can all do about this daunting picture, but this much I do know: The threat of a nuclear holocaust could be significantly reduced if not altogether eliminated by "shut[ting] it down now." Viable plans, and supplies, to protect Americans against smallpox and other dreaded infectious diseases must be put in place now. And government needs to be honest with, and accountable to, all of its citizens, now.

Complacency ended for most of us on September 11, 2001, if not on January 20, when the Bush administration came into power. Now a new kind of vigilance is called for. We must be wary, not only of external forces who would do us ill but of anyone powerful enough to do harm in less obviously catastrophic ways. All this makes for a sad commentary on contemporary life. But better vigilance now than victimization later, no matter what quarter it comes from.

ON BECOMING
AN ELDER

With a significant birthday looming on my horizon, I will soon become what the United Nations officially calls "elderly," although, upon reaching 60, I hope to be known as the noun (Elder) and not the UN's somewhat premature adjective. I do not feel in the least bit elderly as we tend to interpret that word, but I love being an Elder, which reminds me of something Brigitte Bardot once said: "It is sad to grow old but nice to ripen."

The world is a ripening place. By 2050, for the first time in human history, there will be more people over 60 than under 14 on earth. This means that the "elderly" will make up 25 percent of the population of many countries, representing an amazing demographic shift that will call for new ways of thinking about who we are and how we live.

Personally, I've had a stronger sense of who I am during the past decade than I ever have before, and I'm certainly living better. In addition to the facts that my children are living independently and that my husband is retired and therefore relaxed and available, we are blessed with good health, great friends, and financial security. Having worked and traveled abroad for many years, I realize, of course, that the vast majority of Elders who live in other countries can't make similar claims; I know that I am reflecting on aging from an extremely privileged perspective. Still, it *is* a time of personal reflection, and one of the things I know is that aside from the autonomy and security I enjoy, I also have mellowed in ways that only another Elder could appreciate.

I've stopped worrying so much about my appearance, for example. I don't mind, at my age, being a size 14 or having salt-and-pepper hair (although thinning does alarm me). I don't become (so easily) depressed when people say things about me that aren't true or nice. Nor do I feel (quite) so inflated when I am flattered. I (nearly) accept the fact that I am unlikely to make history or to be remembered for great deeds. I am outrageously honest, recalling with quiet pleasure what a friend once told me when she turned 70: "I've finally reached the age when I can do and say what the hell I want!" she said. That thought was deliciously liberating then, as acting upon it is now.

Among the Elders who understand where I'm coming from, to use today's vernacular, are my beloved Crones—a group of women I've been hanging out with for years now. (Three of us go back to junior high school days). A lot of people don't understand why we, like many women entering the third stage of our lives, embrace that word. In their minds, a crone is a haggard old witch incapable of positive action, not someone to be identified with by any stretch. Well, I hate to say so, but we know better. Crones are wise women, elders revered in ancient times for their knowing ways, their healing powers, and their sound judgments. My gang has all those attributes, and they are also the funniest women I've ever known. We laugh ourselves silly when we gather, which we do at least three times a year in various parts of the country. We hike, raft, ride horses, sightsee, shop, eat, do book sales, movies, and much more together. We also reflect upon our lives, share our successes and travails, and support and encourage each other. In 2003 we will begin celebrating our 60 birthdays in each other's company. Sobering though that may seem to all of us at times, we appreciate the wisdom of Mark Twain: Growing older may not be so great until we consider the alternative.

Betty Friedan once said that when her friends threw her a 60th birthday party, she could have killed them all. Not me. I fully expect a huge blast of recognition for having achieved that milestone; I will be terribly disappointed if there isn't resounding fanfare on the occasion! After all, it takes a long time and a lot of experience to become an Elder, and for the first time in my liberal life, I may actually become part of a majority. What's more, I've earned every one of those AARP perqs, and I intend to enjoy each and every one of them.

Such anticipation may not be what the United Nations would call a "senior moment." But to a Crone like me, being an Elder means not only that I've survived, but that I've arrived. The moment is fast approaching when I can finally "say and do whatever the hell I want." So here's my advice for those who may be a bit stunned by their own impending 60th: *Carpe Diem!* As one sage philosopher noted, "age is nothing but a number." To put it another way, as Billie Burke did, "Unless you're a cheese, age doesn't matter." Now there was one smart Elder.

NET GAINS

If you're anything like me, you can't stand to let a telephone ring unanswered. I know people who can do that, and in a way I admire them; it takes a certain kind of self-assurance to feel confident that "if it's important, they'll call back." I'm too curious, and too much of a worrier not to run for the receiver before the fourth ring, upon which my answering system will know who called before I do.

It's the same with mail. There are people who can let a week's worth of envelopes sit unopened on their desks. That really impresses me. I had a boss once who filled her top drawer with still-sealed mail until she felt good and ready to get to it. Not me. I tear the envelopes open before I even leave the post office. Mail is a highlight of my day, and I'm deeply disappointed when all it has to offer is junk and bills. I remember when my kids were little and the biggest event of my life on any given weekday was often the trip to the mailbox. Who knew what resided there to break the monotony of diapers and drool? While Sunday was a day of rest, for me it was also a day of deprivation; mail was my fragile connection to the outside world.

Now the Internet provides an amazing way to interact

with that world. True to form, I am usually compelled to read my e-mail at least once a day, which I struggle to reduce to twice a week if I'm traveling. The problem is, cyber-mail comes with its own unique set of challenges. On a typical day, I might get, say, 40 messages, about 28 of which I don't need or want to read. I can easily delete about two dozen of these. They usually have to do with "Sweet Babes" or interest rates or auto insurance. But several others intrigue me. The subject line says things like "How are you?" or "Thinking of you." Then I need to decide whether to risk contamination because of my overwhelming curiosity. Or messages are often forwarded by friends, and I dare not delete without giving them my full attention. These are the real sticklers. For the most part, they don't come from what Thomas Friedman has called "the sewer of unfiltered information," like the ones that have been circulating for months purporting that NPR is about to be defunded or that if you use the wrong deodorant or underwear you will succumb to cancer. Often the messages that have been passed along ask for action. As an activist, it's hard not to "click here" to be counted. Sometimes they plead for help in finding a lost child (these usually come with a heart-rending picture attached). I got a request recently from a New Zealand fourth-grader whose class was mapping all the places their e-mail had reached. How can you not "reply" and "forward" when it takes so little to make a kid happy?

Still, there's a limit to how much time you can commit to the Information Age. Like everyone else, I'm on overload as it is. It's astonishing, but I find myself not wanting to talk on the phone so much, and on rare occasions, I've actually let a letter sit for a day before reading it. I'm increasingly impatient with the amount of incoming "spam" when I log on, and I've stopped letting people know that in actual fact, underwire brassieres are totally harmless. My activist clicks and charitable responses are diminishing. In short, I seem to be experiencing a technology-induced personality change.

In my case, this may be a good thing: A little less compulsion is probably in order. But what are the larger ramifications? Perhaps too much of a good thing—in this case, information—is bad for us.

The question, of course, is entirely rhetorical: The last thing I want is to hear from anyone on the subject. Except maybe on Sundays. That's the one day of the week when I still think a phone call or a message from "A Friend" would be nice, even if I'm really not interested in Viagra, vision quests, or the geographical efforts of kids from down under.

PROMISING TO LOVE, HONOR, AND STAY

Having just celebrated my 30th wedding anniversary, which in today's world is definitely a minority experience, I was interested to learn that an increasing number of couples are choosing to bypass matrimony as they bond and have families together.

In Norway, for example, nearly 50 percent of all births in 1999 were to unwed parents. In Iceland, the figure was a whopping 62 percent, and even conservative Britain has a rate of 38 percent. In deeply Catholic Ireland, some 31 percent of births in 1999 took place out of wedlock, which is on a par with the U.S. Ireland is unusual: In traditionally religious countries, few children are born to unmarried partners. In 1998 the rate in Italy was 9 percent.

What accounts for this growing trend? Demographers and other social scientists posit that changing attitudes toward religion, family, and the role of the state have made a difference. Marriage is seen as deeply personal, and, for many, obsolete, although most people still marry at some point in their lives. French sociologist Claude Martin, quoted in the

International Herald Tribune (March 25, 2002), thinks that "there is very little difference between being married and cohabitating" in the eyes of most Europeans. With many government officials and some royals in Europe openly living with their partners of choice without benefit of clergy, there would seem to be a consensus on that point, despite efforts in Britain and America to link welfare benefits to family structure. (Interesting to note, then, that two aides to British Prime Minister Tony Blair and his wife Cherie have three children together and are listed in *Who's Who* as "partners.")

Some of my best friends, as the cliche goes, have been cohabitating and raising children together for years. (Most people assume they are married.) One couple in Norway has just celebrated the marriage of a daughter, who took such a drastic step only because she was entering the Foreign Service and couldn't take a boyfriend with her. Another couple adopted a little boy from Mexico nine years ago, and another is celebrating, *Brady Bunch* style, the birth of several grandchildren. So it is not just young pups choosing this more liberated lifestyle. For many who came of age in the 1960s or later, the arrangement seems to suit them best economically and psychologically. All of my friends taking this path have been married before and consider it unnecessarily binding and pretty toxic. They value their independence and feel that their relationships are less precarious, ironically, because they cannot be taken for granted.

Of all the couples I know who live together, none was stronger than my brother and his partner, who shared their lives for 10 years before he passed away. Theirs was a true bond, and even though not overtly romantic (she slept in ratty old flannel nightgowns and wool socks), it always seemed to me that they were on a perpetual date. Childless by choice, they ate by candlelight with fresh flowers on the table, took long weekends away, kept separate bank accounts, and relished each other's company. That's not so likely when you are raising kids together, but there is something special about people who stay together because that's really where they want to be.

I want to be where I am too, but who's to say what might have been if social norms had been different back in 1972? (I certainly would have kept my own name, not to mention my credit cards.) To me, the trend toward cohabitation is a healthy one: I've always thought it should be harder to get married and easier to get divorced. There is, and ought to be, great diversity in what constitutes a family in today's complex world. And it's always wise to "try before you buy." Certainly, welfare policy should ensure that all children have the same financial benefits and treatment, regardless of whether their parents are married, living together, separated, divorced, single, or gay.

So count me among those who are glad for such an enlightened trend in this fragile, fin de siècle world. My husband, by the way, agrees. That's just one of the many reasons I decided to marry him after all.